Flawless Computing

A realistic way to set up your computer for perfect everyday operation

For small business computer users

John Bridges

authorHOUSE™

1663 Liberty Drive, Suite 200
Bloomington, Indiana 47403
(800) 839-8640
www.AuthorHouse.com

First published by AuthorHouse 11/28/05

ISBN: 1-4259-0626-5 (e)
ISBN: 1-4208-8863-3 (sc)

Library of Congress Control Number: 2005908991

Printed in the United States of America
Bloomington, Indiana

This book is printed on acid-free paper.

Introduction

There was a computer shop next door to my office for a long time.   Its business name was Compute This!! #@$%*!!. It was a great takeoff on some old cartoons about users' absolute frustration with computing.

Do you ever feel this way?

It's a rough world out here for non-experts who try to use computers daily to get work done.   Unpredictable things happen constantly.   It sometimes seems that we fight our computers more than we use them to actually get work done.

The purpose of this book is to show you a specific Process or Method for setting up your computer so that it works perfectly in this real-world environment, essentially until the hardware fails.

The goals here are to describe the problem in detail and to convince you that there is in fact a realistic solution.   We will then lay out the details for applying this solution to your computer.

The solution is not a piece of cleanup software, spyware removal software, virus scanner, or firewall.

The solution is a Process which will bring your computer back to pure quickly, no matter what happens.

I had some trepidations about writing this, and it took me a while to figure out the reason.

Simply, I have many friends who are programmers and/or other forms of experts who would consider this entire thing almost insultingly simplistic. The fundamental ideas (partitioning and imaging) are well known, have been around for some time, and are widely used by knowledgeable individuals. Universities, network managers, hardware vendors who produce many copies of identical machines, and other individuals routinely use imaging and cloning software to maintain their environments.

But I also have many other friends and customers who are quite computer literate, who make expert use of Excel, Powerpoint and other programs daily, who have simply never been shown anything like this process, and who suffer through needless grief and pain trying to get work done.

Programmers, IT staff, and experts are not the audience for which this is written. It is for the larger number of generally computer knowledgeable individuals who are not experts, who need their computers to function reliably every day, and who fight unknown and unknowable problems while trying to simply get their work done.

Our target here is the Small Office business computer user who is reasonably computer literate, and to whom the computer is an integral part of the everyday work being performed.

We will show you a process that really works, revolving around the concept of "imaging" a partition on your hard disk. To be clear again, the concept is not new, nor is it original with us – software which performs this imaging function has been available for some time and from several vendors.

Also to be clear, this method will not protect from 100% of occurrences - in an extreme example if someone attacks your machine with a hammer no one can protect against that. However, what we *can* say is that if you apply this method then you realistically will have ability to recover quickly, even in these extreme situations.

We will give very specific, detailed instructions on a Process that will work for you if your machine is critical to your business.

The key is the phrase "reasonably computer literate" individual.

Suppose the average user reads instructions like "...should work with SCSI and IDE writers produced in 2000 or later. It may or may not work with older models. Use the latest firmware available for your CD/DVD writer. An IDE CD/DVD writer performs best if it is mounted on the secondary IDE controller...."

Eyes will glaze over. More importantly, there is just no way that the average individual can understand what is going on, nor will they be willing to risk their machine crashing by actually trying a process described in this way.

The problem is that most programmers and IT people just cannot speak normal English. That is, they assume that everyone else understands systems as well as they do, and can't bring the instructions "down" to where a normal intelligent user can understand them.

We will try to do that for you.

The basic sections of this volume are:
> The modern computing environment – it's worse than you might think.
> Why your machine degrades – and why it's unavoidable.
> The basic concepts of partitioning, imaging, and user files
> The Solution Process
> How to apply the Process

Bon reading!

Table of Contents

Chapter 1 –

Computing In The Real World

The owner of my office complex comes up to me in a panic – "My Outlook address book just vanished!! Some of those addresses are impossible to recover….What do I do?!??"

My brother calls me – "My Front Page just stopped working!!"

I call my Accountant. He is behind on doing my taxes this year. A virus wiped out his machines the first week of April (terrible timing!). Yes, he had a very well-known brand of anti-virus software installed.

A lawyer in the office around the corner grabbed me – he had been fooled a month ago by a pop-up box saying that a Microsoft Security Update was ready to be installed. It was a worm that destroyed many of his files. Now he had another similar box on his screen. It sure looked like Microsoft, but what should he do? He was legitimately afraid to touch it.

A friend of mine called me for help. He had a four-month old machine, with a fast processor and lots of memory. It had slowed to a crawl, and he was being barraged by pop-up ads. Everything, even turning the machine on, was taking forever. Something was wrong.

On and on…..

All true stories. And that's just in one week. Most of you could fill in a few dozen examples of your own.

You are a home user, or a small office user. You have one or two machines, or maybe three or four employees with machines. The computer is critical to you. However, you do not have access to an expert IT staff as in a larger firm. You are not an expert, and neither are your employees.

You don't have time to learn to be an expert, either – you're too busy doing accounting, real estate, office management, or whatever you do for a living.

Problems keep happening for no apparent reason.

What do you do?

Why the Problem Exists

A Windows system, fresh out of the box, brand new, probably works very well barring a rare manufacturer's defect.

However, it doesn't stay that way forever.

Essentially, every use of the computer takes it further down the path towards instability. The user installs software to do various functions. The user plays games, browses the internet, gets and sends email.

Then things start to happen. SuperWonderful Bar!!! (which I never asked for) shows up on my Internet Explorer. A strange blue bar with a porno link appears, and presents me with constant porno ads – I didn't ask for this! I'm barraged with ads.

Things stop working, for no apparent reason, taking seemingly forever to resolve.

The machine gets slower and slower, and that fast new computer you bought grinds to a crawl.

As I am writing this section, my brother calls me – "My Front Page stopped working! Grrrrrr!!" Why? Who knows? He'll spend all day trying to figure it out, or maybe just save some files and re-install Front Page. Maybe that will work, maybe not. Even if it works, whatever corruption caused the failure is probably still there. And of course there is the time involved in saving things (hopefully the right things) and putting them back once Front Page is reinstalled and (hopefully) working. This will be time consuming and confusing, of course, as it is often not clear to the average user what to save, how to save it, and how exactly to put it back.

Things like this keep happening. As time goes on, the machine finally becomes too unstable to be usable or slows to a crawl. One option at that point is to go buy another machine, and the sequence starts all over again. Or we take it to a repair shop and pay an expert to figure out what's wrong and restore it to usability for a while. Or we find a friendly nerd to help out, and hope that he/she actually knows what to do – since all computer experts seem to speak this strange language, it's impossible to tell if they actually know what they are doing or not. So we just muddle along.

I showed a draft of this book to my accountant. We were sitting in his conference room discussing it. He pointed to the sides of the room – lining the walls were several old machines no longer in use. The hardware still worked, but they had become so degraded that the only option seemed to be to purchase new machines, which he had done.

Chapter 2 –

Specific Problems

Here are some of the problems in today's real-world environment:

Viruses, Worms, Trojans

Everyone knows about these – they're well publicized.

What you may not know is that you can get a virus even if you have well-known and functioning anti-virus software installed. When a new virus appears in the world, it takes a period of time (often at least a day or two after it becomes known) for the anti-virus firms to become aware of the virus, then to obtain a copy of the virus, determine its characteristics, and modify their anti-virus setups to deal with the new attack. During that period of time you are vulnerable, even with well-known and reputable anti-virus software vendors.

Adware, Spyware and other "Malware"

There is another growing type of problem software generally called "spyware", "adware", or more generally "malware". This has become huge.

The mildest forms of this software log your internet activity so marketing can build databases of user activity, thus allowing advertising to be directed at you specifically or so that advertising may be better targeted.

The more dangerous programs of this type can log every keystroke you make, stealing passwords and credit card information, which is then "sent home" to the spyware maker.

Some software of this type actually takes over your machine and uses your machine to send spam to millions of other computers, without your knowledge. More than one computer user has had his or her internet account terminated because, to their complete surprise, millions of spam emails had been sent from their machine.

These things always come into your machine surreptitiously, and do not show in your add/remove program list. They operate invisibly in the background.

Often the user (particularly a child) is tricked into installing this software by offering games, cool mouse cursors, screen savers, or other innocent-appearing items. However, even aware adults can be tricked. Do you know those license boxes that you routinely agree to (and never read) when you install something? Many of those licenses tell you in English (buried in the part no one reads) something on the order of "we are about to install advertising software which logs your internet activity". Since it is being honest and up-front (even though no one ever reads the license agreement), such software is not classified as a "virus", and is not removed by many programs.

One major anti-virus vendor started using the phrase "potentially unwanted program" (PUP) to describe these programs, instead of "spyware", to avoid potential legal problems with individuals who say in effect "we tell the user what we are going to do, so we are not producing spyware".

It is possible for this software to creep into your machine without you doing anything at all, although these can be labeled viruses, worms, or trojans. It gets to be a matter of language, but frankly as a user I don't care what it's called - it's going to cause me problems.

Spyware makers are becoming more and more clever – they can hide copies of themselves on your machine, so that they can reinstall themselves even after removal by anti-spyware software.

From PC World magazine, July 2004, p. 36:

"Spyware's recent spread has been breathtaking. Network monitoring firm Websense found spyware on 92 percent of PCs in an April study of firms with more than 100 employees. Microsoft blames spyware for over half of all application crashes. An analysis by Earthlink/Webroot eports an average of 28 spyware programs it scanned for a recent study."

P. 49, same issue: "...users are being plagued by an infestation of bogus anti-spyware apps, which claim to remove spyware but in reality embed the nasty stuff in your computer. ... Unsuspecting users are suckered by dire warnings that their system could be attacked by spyware."

This happened to me. I was testing a certain anti-virus and firewall combination, and something called SearchBar magically appeared above the taskbar on my machine, with a permanent sign promising "Free $$$" right in the middle staring at me at all times, and with "Bargain Buddy" rotating ads over on the right. I had not downloaded anything, nor had I opened any email attachments, nor had I said "yes" to any screens. It just appeared.

The builders of this malware are playing "no holds barred" in attacking your machine. If you click on a button that says "free scan for spyware", you might be installing spyware, not removing it.

The more subtle forms of this malware are hard to detect other than noticing a general slowness of your machine.

This has become a very popular cause for software vendors. I am barraged with spyware cleanup ads every time I use Internet Explorer lately. I even saw an anti-spyware software advertisement on ESPN during work on a draft of this manuscript.

Therefore, I do not want to overemphasize this particular problem, bad as it is, for this reason: the reader might get the impression that buying a spyware/adware removal package is the only thing that's needed, and the real-world problem is much deeper than this.

Multiple Software Vendors.

We all use various software applications to perform various tasks. These software applications make various changes to your machine as they are installed and used. Since humans are imperfect and since perfect coordination among software vendors is impossible, problems are certain even with reliable, solid vendors with good reputations and good intentions.

And, frankly, some vendors are simply not that good.

Windows Itself

Windows is complicated. It has bugs, security holes, and flaws. That's why there are frequent security releases, updates, and "Service Packs".

A typical Windows security update has something like this in its description: "A security issue has been identified that could allow an attacker to compromise a computer and gain complete control over it." This is common language. Security flaws of this type are being discovered frequently, meaning that they exist in your machine right now.

If the virus or worm or trojan is taking advantage of a windows security flaw it may take some period of time for Microsoft to analyze and issue a patch for that security flaw. This is an entirely broader subject than we are prepared to address here, but needless to say these vulnerabilities allow bad things to happen to your machine, no matter how careful you are, and no matter how good your anti-virus and firewall software are.

Microsft is doing much better in this area, as evidenced by the release of XP Serivce Pack 2 and its followups. However, the problem is fundamentally not solvable. The only way to absolutely guarantee 100% complete security for a machine is to turn it off. Since you must allow some communication with the outside world in order to get work done, there will always be ways for appropriately evil individuals to achieve their ends, <u>especially on home or small office machines where security experts are not available to watch every move and set up every system detail.</u>

Inside Your Machine

This section might be overkill, but we consider it important to illustrate the complexity of what is going on inside your machine. There is a file called the Registry, which contains tens of thousands of entries which Windows refers to constantly in order to function.

This is a picture of one tiny piece of the Registry:

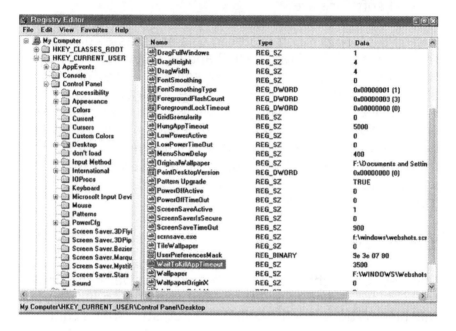

This is actually one of the more readable portions of the Registry – some sections are absolute gobbledygook to anyone but an expert.

In the highlighted example, the Registry is telling Windows to wait a certain period of time before killing an Application due to timeout. Up above, you will see that it says the Screen Saver is Active, that we should not Tile Wallpaper, that we should wait a certain period of time before killing a hung application, on and on.

There are tens of thousands of entries in this system file, and many are so delicate that a single incorrect character will cause Windows to fail. This is why every recommended action involving the Registry is preceded by an extremely strong warning to back up your Registry.

The reason for showing you the above is this: every installation of every piece of software makes registry changes as it is installed. Every installation also adds files to your system, and makes other changes. Since there are so many of these items, and since they are so complicated and delicate, every installation of any piece of software has the potential to take your system further down the road of degradation.

Recall from the above discussion of "malware" that malicious software of this type installs itself on your machine without your knowledge. Individuals producing this type of software, being illegitimate and shady in the first place, have no interest whatsoever in taking measures to keep your machine stable.

Uninstalls

Uninstalls are another problem. Just because you have uninstalled a piece of software does not mean it is completely gone. Consider a common example – instant messaging software. I installed a well-known and widely used instant messenger on my machine, and then did an uninstall. I then manually counted 168 references to this piece of software remaining in my Registry after the uninstall, in addition to a directory still living on the hard drive. Over time, as software is installed and uninstalled this clutter accumulates, and contributes to system instability.

The messenger I tested is from a well-known and reputable software vendor, but how many software applications are built by less well-known or reputable vendors, whose programmers may or may not be taking all the necessary precautions against destabilizing your system?

Kids and Family

If your work machine is in your home, there may be no practical way to prevent your family from using the machine for normal purposes.

One of my best customers recently called me for help. He had to do a complete reinstall of my software. He was, in fact, almost "rebuilding" his machine, because, to use his words, "little hands" had gotten on the machine. This is not uncommon, and realistically it's not preventable.

Overall

Without exaggeration, it is fair to say that literally every use of your machine takes you further down the road to destabilization. Every install, uninstall, or internet use introduces some risk of degradation and instability into your world.

These accumulate over time, and it's unavoidable.

Chapter 3 –

The Role of the User

Part of the problem is, unfortunately, a misconception on the part of the user.

The user image typically is that the computer is like a TV set. You buy a TV set, plug it in, turn it on, and use it without any problem. When you buy a TV you do not expect to also buy $200 worth of maintenance items and spend an hour or two every week maintaining it. It's supposed to just work.

The industry of course wanted the computer to operate in this manner, but it hasn't worked out that way.

This analogy is unfortunately incorrect in the modern environment. The computer realistically is much more like a house. You not only expect to pay for ongoing maintenance and repairs, but you expect to have to learn how to do some things yourself. Mow the yard, fix a door handle, do minor plumbing repairs, etc. depending on your level of skill.

I am going to present a methodology for keeping your computer in absolutely perfect working order in this real-world, very nasty and complicated environment. The house analogy will apply in the sense that you will have to obtain and learn how to use some tools, and will spend some money and more importantly some *time* on maintenance.

If you can adopt a mentality that the computer is like a car or a house, and in your mind allow for some cost per year for maintenance and a modicum of time spent every few days maintaining it, then there is a way to make the computer work first time, every time, reliably, every time you turn it on, and to recover back to perfect in minutes from any problem. Gone will be porn, SuperDuper Bar, the latest virus problem, spyware, or problems with that program that just stopped for no apparent reason.

You can make it so that you can recover your machine in a few minutes no matter what your kids, the neighbor kids, or some extremely clever hackers do to it. When CNN is saying that the Bugaboo virus is destroying machines all over the world, you can have a glass of milk and go to bed. All is well.

I told my wife, and meant it: "You cannot hurt this machine."

She didn't believe me at first – she is fairly much a computer novice, and was afraid to touch our home computer because she knew I use it for my work. She was afraid that she was going to accidentally damage or erase something important. Now she is convinced, because it is true. She cannot hurt that machine, period. My granddaughter plays on the machine, too. She can't hurt it either.

If the computer is critically important to you, as it is to me, then it is worth your time and money to do this. I have been doing this Process to all my machines for a few years now, and although I confess to saying a bad word or two when problems happen, recovery is trivial.

There is an important implication here which is worth discussing at more length. The assumption is that you are a small or medium business user with the characteristic that the data on your machine or the ability to operate that machine perfectly every day has *value* to your business.

How much value did the lost time have for my lawyer friend who spent six weeks recovering from a worm? How much value did the lost time and effort have for my accountant who spent two months recovering from a virus? How much value did the lost time and data have for my tennis pro friend, who had a virus wipe out all his payroll records, club membership lists, and tournament entries? Put any realistic number on these incidents, and it's not hard in most cases to come up with a value in four or five figures that is not out of line.

The implication is this: We are going to give specific instructions on how to set up a Process that really works. It is going to cost you some money and time, and it probably will cost you some learning curve effort to learn some different or new software, and to modify your approach to computing.

That is on purpose, and should be expected. There is a cost, in time, in money, and in rearranged use of the computer.

The last item – rearranged use of the computer – is in practice something of a hurdle. I, for one, am a creature of habit as I get older, and rearranging the way in which I use a computer is not painless. It's much like asking me to rearrange my eating or sleeping habits. But it is possibly the most critical part of the process. It would be nice if some $39 software package could solve all these problems, but life isn't that easy.

There is no free lunch.

There is no magic piece of cleanup software that will make everything right.

What I will do is recommend to you a set of hardware, software, tools, and operating arrangements that will work. It has worked for me extremely well. In fact, I will say that it has worked absolutely flawlessly for me for a very long time. If your data and time have genuine value, you will find these costs of money , time, and rearranged work habits more than worthwhile.

Chapter 4 –

Basic Concepts I - The two types of files

We start with the three basic concepts necessary for understanding the Process and why it works.

I will use as an example my accounting software – Quickbooks. This is an accounting package for small businesses.

> Most users visualize a program in a computer as a single "thing." It is not.

As with most software packages, you open Quickbooks and are able then to perform various work activities. In this case, I click on a company name, and various things appear with a number of options, allowing me to work with that company data – payroll, banking, paying bills, etc.

A co-worker in my office building refers to one of her machines as "my Quickbooks machine", meaning that it's the machine she uses to do the accounting and invoicing. In her mind Quickbooks is a single unit.

It is not a single unit.

In actuality there are two separate things on your computer:

1. The files required for Quickbooks itself to operate.
2. The accounting files for the company being worked on.

That is, for each application program you use there are

1. Program Files
2. User Files

The Program Files are fixed and don't change very often – generally, only when some update of the program itself is done, as in the release of a new version or installation of new features or upgrades.

The User Files will change typically every day, as the system is used.

This is a picture of the Quickbooks directory on my machine:

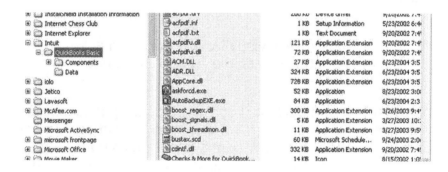

Notice the long list of files on the right. There are too many to show all at one time – you are looking only at a few. These are files required for Quickbooks itself to run. On my machine, the Quickbooks directory has 3,409 files and 202 directories or folders containing the files required for Quickbooks to operate. These are installed when I install Quickbooks.

However, the User Data files, which actually contain my accounting information, are totally separate. There are only <u>two</u> files on my machine which actually contain my accounting information and user data. I have two companies, so (without being specific) the only two files which ever change as I use Quickbooks are:

XYZ Company.qbw   and
ABC Company.qbw

The "qbw" on the end tells the system this is a QuickBooks Works file. All the other files besides these two remain stable, and never change.

What we are going to do is separate these two types of files, putting the program files in one place (which we are going to keep pure and stable) while placing the User Files elsewhere.

Microsoft went this direction partially, when for example it placed your Microsoft Office user files in a directory called My Documents. This is not physically the place where Microsoft Word itself is installed.

Those who work in corporations with networks are probably familiar with the concept: It is common to have, say, Microsoft Word on your machine accessing documents which are physically on a computer somewhere else on the network.

We are just going to take this concept one step further, and apply it to a single machine in a small office environment.

Chapter 5 –

Basic Concepts II - Partitioning

Most users have their hard disk drive structured in a single unit, called the "C" Drive.

A picture would look like this:

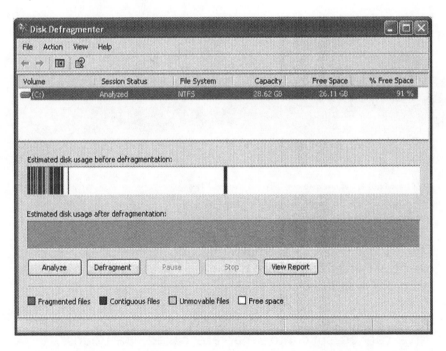

This is a picture of a fresh Windows XP install, with the dark lines representing the files and programs installed on the hard drive. This particular hard drive has 30 gigabytes on it, usually written as 30GB. This is roughly 30 billion bytes.

Without going into too much detail for novices, a byte is enough space to hold one character of information.

Notice that most of the drive is empty. In most machines, over time this free space is filled with documents, accounting files, pictures, music, and so on, as the user makes use of the computer for various functions.

The drive ends up looking like this:

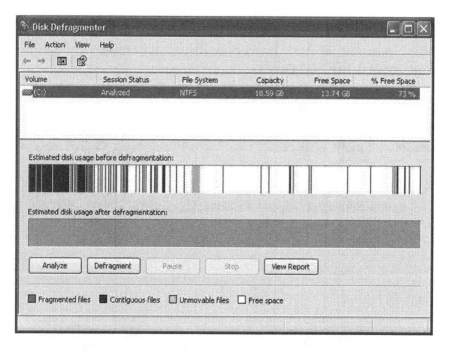

The C: drive now has many files on it, which are spread over the hard drive. Note that much space in this particular example is still empty.

Many regular users do not know that the physical hard drive can be split into what are called "partitions". A typical machine arrives with the entire hard disk installed into one "partition", called the "C: Drive." The "C:" is the conventional way of denoting the partition. Pictorially, the C: partition takes up the entire hard drive:

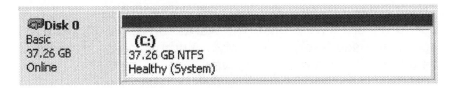

What we are going to do is split the hard disk into two partitions, the C: drive, and the D: drive, like this:

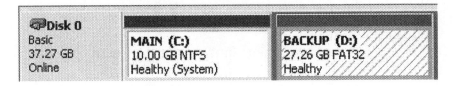

In this example, the physical hard drive is split into two partitions: the C: partition with 10 Gigabytes and the D: partition with 27.2 Gigabytes of spade. Notice that each partition has a letter designation and a name.

The C: drive in this example has the name "MAIN" and the D: drive in this particular example is named "BACKUP." The assigned names are arbitrary, and in many cases the letter designation (e.g., the "D:" partition) is arbitrary also.

Many advanced users do this in order to better organize their information. When the hard drive is split into partitions each new partition is named with a letter. Thus a partitioned hard disk might look like the following:

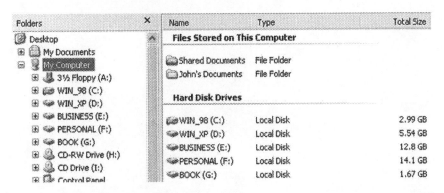

This is my primary working machine. There are five partitions or "drives" on it (the words "drive" and "partition" are often used interchangeably). Without going into detail as to why it's organized this way, I have

1. The C: drive running Windows 98
2. The D: drive running Windows XP Pro
3. The E: drive containing my documents and other business files
4. The F: drive containing some club minutes, music, and photographs
5. The G: drive containing files associated with this book project.

Note that I have two CD drives on this machine: a CD burner (named with the letter "H") and an ordinary CD drive (named with the letter "I").

These letter assignments are somewhat arbitrary, and may be different on a particular machine. The naming ("Business", "Personal", etc.) is also completely arbitrary, and will be different on different machines.

Partitioning in this manner can be used to better organize the literally tens of thousands of files that appear on the computer over time. We are going to use this partitioning for an additional purpose.

Chapter 6 –

Basic Concepts III - Imaging

Assume now that you have divided your hard drive into two or more sections, which are called "partitions."

There are a number of vendors who produce software which can make an exact "Image" of a partition of a hard drive. These are sometimes called "ghost" or "mirror" or "cloned" images. We will use the term "image" in this context.

> These special purpose programs make an
> exact, sector-for-sector copy of the C: drive,
> and put that image in a file somewhere else.

In my case, I put it on my "E:" drive (and later, as we will describe, copy it to a writable DVD).

Note what this does and does not do.

You could not achieve the same effect by simply copying all the files on the C: partition somewhere else. This would not work if you as an end user tried to do it. Even if you could copy all the files and system areas, the system would not let you simply copy them back later – they are protected on purpose for obvious reasons – a user touching many of these files and areas could crash the entire system easily.

You need special software built for this purpose.

Pictorially, we are going to make a "mirror" image of the <u>entire</u> C: partition and place it in that image in a file on the D: partition, like this:

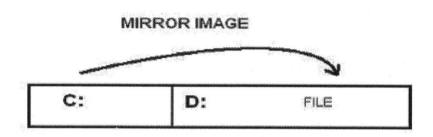

MIRROR IMAGE

Many programs serve the function of "recovery" or "backup and recovery" tools, but do not really do this function. Rather, they do a partial backup and restore of certain selected files and settings.

Windows System Restore, as an example of a partial recovery method, does a "backup" and then a "restore", but only of certain selected files and settings, not everything on the partition. It cannot do more because it would overwrite documents you have stored on the C: drive, which would erase all your recent work. Windows System Restore attempts to bring your machine back to usability when there are problems without destroying the user files we have been discussing. Therefore, it may or may not fix an actual problem you have, and is not even intended to clean out all spyware or viruses from a system.

Partial recovery software of this type cannot bring your machine back to perfect, because it does not know what "perfect" was.

The imaging software to which we are referring makes an exact copy of the entire drive, literally "sector for sector." The methods vary somewhat depending on the software vendor, but the result is the same.

The same software that made the image of the partition can reverse the process, copying that file back onto the partition that was imaged, making that partition identical, sector for sector, to what it was when it was imaged.

By using compression, the copy will take less space, but when restored later, you will have your entire C: drive in exactly the form in which it was copied, with literally zero changes.

Chapter 7 –

Combining it all – The Process

Here is what I do with a new machine.

a) First, I split the hard drive into two (or more) partitions.

Most computer users (as described above) have their hard drive in one single unit: the C: drive. Let us assume that you have split the hard drive into two separate partions: the C: drive and the D: drive (the letters may be a bit different on any particular machine). At any rate, split the hard drive – I will assume the drives are labeled C: and D: in the rest of this manuscript.

b) I put 5 gigabytes into C: and the rest into D.

The C drive is relatively small on purpose, since it will contain only the programs that I use, and none of the user data. You may have to make this partition somewhat larger, but generally make it as small as possible (see later chapters for details).

c) I install all my programs and operating system onto the C: drive as usual.

d) I then arrange so that all the data being used by those programs is on the D: drive.

That is, all the programs are on C: and all the documents, accounting files, email files, and every other file that is in use by those programs is over on D:. We called these the "User Files" above.

Pictorially for, say, Microsoft Word, we will have the program installed and operating on the C: Drive, and the Documents (User Files) all physically on the D: drive, like this:

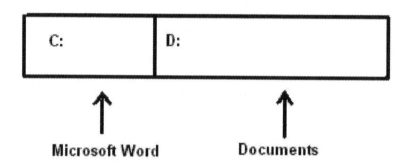

We will describe later how to move the User Files for various applications, particularly Microsoft Office and Microsoft Outlook.

Rationale: Viruses, corrupted registries, poor uninstalls, spyware, pornographic adware, etc. all generally affect only the working drive, which is usually the "C:" drive. We are going to making a mirror image of the C: drive so that you can restore the C: drive back to perfect quickly, wiping out any corruption or undesirable changes, while leaving your actual data alone.

e) Having set up my hard drive in this manner, I make an image of the C: drive and put it on the D: drive.

f) I copy that image onto a writable DVD.

What we have done is put all the Program Files on the C drive and all the User Data files on other drives. I can now image the C: drive for later retrieval, use my programs as I want, and whenever I wish bring my C: drive back to a perfect, pure state.

So here, in more detail, is my process for setting up a new machine (assume XP is freshly installed):

1. Before doing anything else, split the hard drive into C and D drives.

2. If the machine came with an operating system (e.g., Windows XP) installed, make an image copy of the C drive as is before doing any changes whatsoever, and put that copy on the D drive. Name this file as "original" or some such name, meaning that you have copied the working installation before you make any changes or added any new software. You can always come back to this pure, original install. (Footnote: be sure to activate your operating system installation prior to making this original image, else it will be unusable later).

3. Install all my office, internet, accounting, email, and other software as usual. In each case, set the application software up so that the actual files in use are over on the D drive, not on the C drive (we describe later how to do this).

Be very sure that all your programs are actually working on data in the D drive, not on the C drive. Test and re-test by creating new documents or other user files and verifying that they actually are ending up on the alternate drive. This is important, as we will be frequently over-writing the contents of the C drive. If you have working email or other files on that drive, they will be erased every time we bring the C drive back to perfect.

4. Do all the appropriate updates from Windows Update.

5. Do standard maintenance – defrag and clean up garbage files. We are going to make this C drive as pure as possible.

6. Now make another image of the C drive, and put it on the D drive. Give this a name with a date. For example, call it MAY1104.BAK. Code it so that you can tell from the filename the date when it was made. This will be useful later.

7. (somewhat optional) Copy this image to a writable DVD. This provides a bulletproof backup in case some serious damage occurs to your hard drive.

Chapter 8 –

When Problems Occur

Restore the image.

As pointed out above, the same software which created the image can restore that image, making the restored drive identical to the point in time at which it was imaged, with literally zero changes.

You are now back to perfect, back to a literally pure working machine.

It's that simple, absolutely no sarcasm intended.

All of the above preparation was so that you could be ready to do this. In a few minutes, you are back to perfect, back to pure. Whatever worked before now works again. Whatever degradation has happened is gone. All is 100% perfect again, quite literally.

Any virus that has crept in, or spyware or adware that has snuck in behind your back, is gone. Any corrupted file is pure again. The registry is now perfect again. All settings are restored. Literally, everything is back to precisely the absolutely perfect state of your new machine.

More importantly, since we have separated the User Files from the actual working programs, none of your recent work is lost when you restore this image.

This restore does not affect your documents, email files, or any other data living on your system, as we have physically moved that to a different partition.

We have restored the system to perfect while retaining all of your recent work.

I actually do this restore every day on one of my machines – there is no reason not to. That way, I start every day with a pure, 100% perfect installation. No degradation. No irritating slowdowns. No unexpected anything. Everything works perfectly. No surprises. I can concentrate on getting my work done.

Chapter 9 –

A Few More Preliminaries

Translating our Directions – Partition Letters and Names

We attempt in this book to show you specific screen sequences for each function we recommend you do, to the degree possible.

There is one area in which the screens you see will probably differ from the screen prints shown in this book, and that is in the naming of partitions. The key fact you need to keep in mind is:

Letter assignments on partitions on your hard drive are often arbitrary – they can be any letter (although the primary or Windows partition is almost always given the letter C:).

Naming of partitions is always arbitrary – they can be quite literally anything.

Do one of the following:

1. If you are using the "classic" XP User Interface, Click on Start, then click on Settings, then click on Control Panel, then click on Administrative Tools, then click on Computer Management, then click on Disk Management.

2. If you are using the newer XP User Interface, then click on Start and then click on Control Panel, then Administrative Tools then Disk Management as above.

You will see a picture something like this:

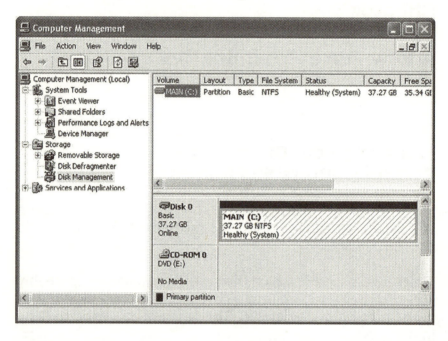

In this example, there is a C: drive which has the name "MAIN", and the C: drive is the only partition on the hard drive.

That name "MAIN" may be anything whatsoever. On some machines it may be called "WINDOWS" or "WIN_XP". It may be any name at all. We could name it "HARRY" or "SUE" if we wished.

If you look at a new Hewlett-Packard machine, same screen, you might see something along these lines:

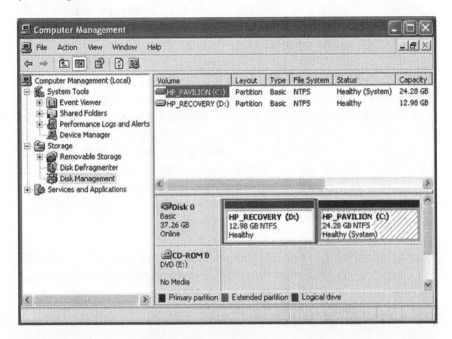

Note that here the vendor has named the C: drive as "HP_PAVILION", since that is the brand of the computer – Pavilion, and of course HP is short for the vendor name – Hewlett Packard.

On a Compaq machine these names might be "PRESARIO" and "PRESARIO_RP", with Presario being the brand name of the computer.

For your machine, you may see any number of names, depending on the choice of names by the particular vendor – Dell, Compaq, Gateway, etc., and depending on the brand name on the machine.

An important note on the last illustration:

There is a partition on the hard drive, which the vendor has given the letter D: and which is called "HP_RECOVERY" and which on a Compaq machine might be called "PRESARIO_RP."

This latter is shorthand for "Presario Recovery Partition." These recovery partitions contain files which serve the purpose, should the machine get too badly corrupted, of allowing the user to take the machine back to original factory delivered condition.

Note that this is, in essence, the process we describing – the machine contains a full image of the original installation for use in emergency recovery. However, there is one huge difference – invoking this recovery partition will make the machine exactly as it came from the factory, thus destroying all your files or other work done since you bought the machine. Although useful in some situations, this too often results in loss of much useful information or files from your recent work.

Sometimes this recovery function is on a CD or DVD delivered with the machine, and sometimes (as here) the recovery function is on the hard drive itself, with access to that recovery available during boot-up of the machine.

We will in this book call the C: partition the "Windows" partition or the "working" partition, as that is the partition where your operating system (Windows XP or Windows 98 etc.) resides. It is also where your registry and Windows settings reside. Advanced users may have this active partition in other places, but for most small-business users the active Windows partition will be the C: drive.

We will create on your hard drive another partition which we will call your "alternate" partition or drive. This is where we will store your user files and images.

It is very important to note that, although the active partition almost always has the letter C: assigned to it, that the alternate partition may be assigned almost any letter whatsoever.

In the above case the vendor has assigned the letter D: to a partition already, using that D: partition as a storage place for recovery files. Your CD and DVD drives (and possibly other devices on your machine) may be occupying letters such as F:, G:, etc. Therefore, when we (using partitioning software) create an another (alternate) partition on your drive we will have to assign it some available letter, and give it a name.

The letter assigned depends on what is available (unused) on your particular machine, and the name is as always completely arbitrary.

> As we show you screen prints for partitioning and imaging software, please translate the partition letters and names to those appropriate for your specific machine.

Final Preliminary – Navigating and Manipulating the Windows File System

In order for you to follow the directions we are about to give you, it is necessary that you take time to learn some basics on navigating and manipulating the Windows file system if you are unfamiliar with it. You must have some understanding of how the files in a Windows computer are organized, and how to move those files around the system.

We are going to ask you to do tasks such as:

1. "Browse" to a certain location (a file or a folder) on your computer

2. Create a new folder

3. Search for a file or folder

4. Move a file or folder from one place to another

5. Combined tasks – for example, find a file and then move it to a different place

If you are unfamiliar with the Windows file system, or if you are not sure how to do any of these tasks, then we suggest you pause now and go read <u>and study</u> Appendix 5 – The Windows File System, A Primer.

These are necessary skills if you want to actually do the process we are describing. Lack of these skills is the biggest single wall between you and effective use of your computer.

Chapter 10 –

How to Do Partitioning

Here is how the partitioning and imaging process works in practice with one of the special-purpose software packages mentioned above. The one illustrated here is called Acronis Disk Director, from www.acronis.com. The following screen prints are from that software package. Full disclosure: the author is an Acronis affiliate.

Be sure to read the following chapters on applying this process in various situations before actually proceeding with this. There are some major footnotes particularly when applying to anything other than a brand new machine.

Note: prior to performing any partitioning process on your hard drive, defragment the data already on that drive. This makes the re-partitioning process much simpler and faster.

To add a new partition on a hard drive you must do the following two steps:

1. Create some free space on the hard drive by resizing an existing partition.

2. Create a new partition in that free space.

Initially the entire hard drive will be allocated to at least one partition, usually the C: partition. In the example shown here we start with a hard drive which has only one partition. Before creating a new partition, we must first make some space for the new partition. Initially, in this example, the hard drive looks like this, with the C: drive taking about 37 gigabytes of space, and taking up the entire hard drive. This is the first screen you will see when starting Disk Director:

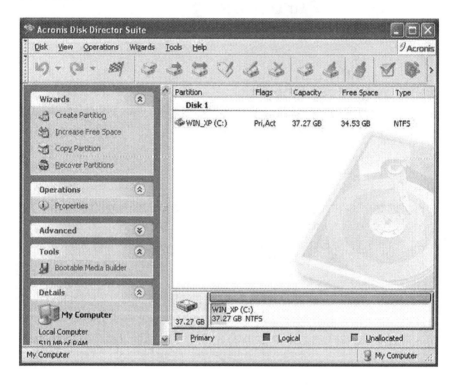

Note that the C: drive in this example is called WIN_XP. As noted above, it may be named something different on your machine.

Clicking on the C: drive (and thus highlighting it) and clicking on "Operations" on the left, brings up a set of operations which may be performed:

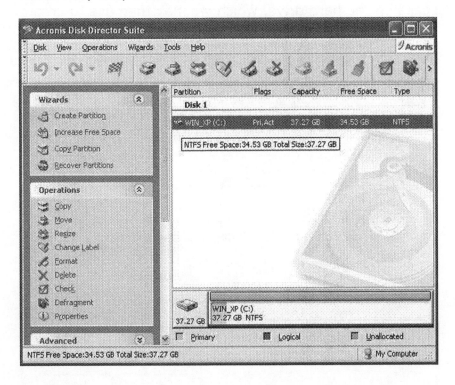

Clicking on "Resize" on the left brings up the following screen. What we are going to do is resize the C: partition, making it smaller. This will create some free or "unallocated" space on the hard drive, which we may then use to create a new partition:

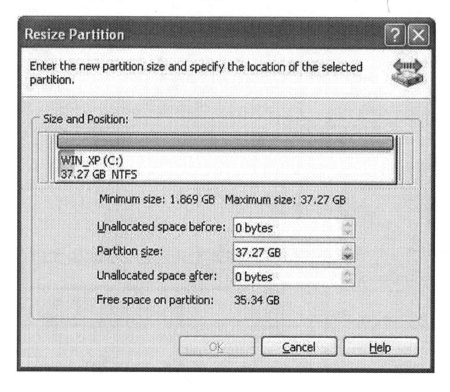

By sliding (with the mouse) the right side of the bar illustrating the C: partition, or by using the numeric Partition Size entry below that, we change the size of the C: drive to approximately 5 gigabytes:

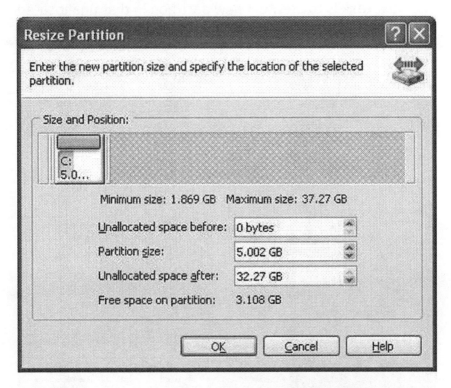

Note the small greyed-in area in the picture of the C: drive. The software is showing that part of the C: drive which is presently in use by files. This is a brand-new XP installation with zero additional software installed, and thus the occupied space is quite small. You cannot make the C: drive smaller than the size of the files physically on it – for example, if you have 8 gigabytes of files on your C: drive, you cannot make the partition smaller than 8 gigabytes.

Now, after clicking OK the software reverts to the original picture – note that we now have a large amount of space on the right which is not allocated to any partition:

Our next task is to create a new partition in that unallocated space. Clicking on the "Unallocated" space produces the following:

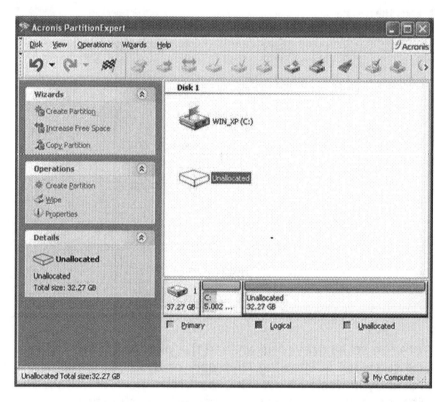

Now, clicking on "Create Partition" we get this screen:

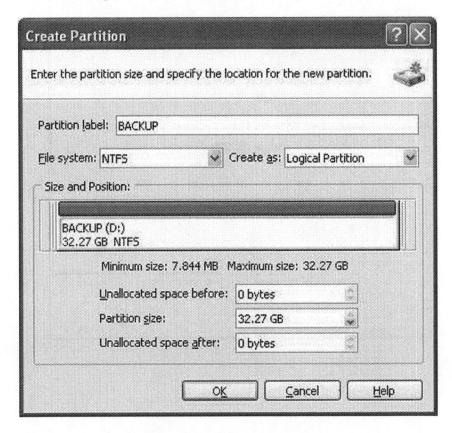

There is no reason not to take defaults on this screen. The NTFS file system is fine, and it is going to be a logical partition. We have chosen the name "BACKUP" for this newly created partition. Recall that this name is arbitrary.

Clicking on OK gives you:

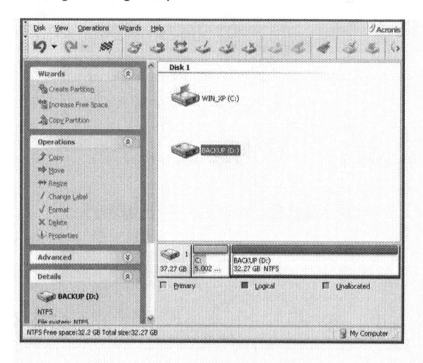

Now, clicking on Operations and then "Commit" tells the software to actually commit to (or apply) the changes you have told it to make:

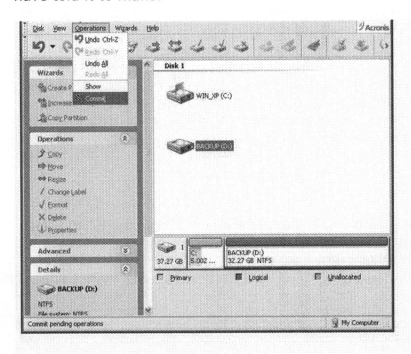

The software will reboot your machine after it completes the partitioning assignments you have given it.

After your machine reboots, Windows XP will observe the changes, and tell you that you need to reboot again. This is normal.

A general observation about partitioning is this: the partitioning of the hard drive is a one-time event. You do it once, and generally will not have to worry about partitions for the life of that machine.

If you are new at doing this process, and since it is a one time event, it might be better for some users to have this partitioning done by a reputable local computer shop, or by an expert friend. This will generally cost you about the same as the cost of partitioning software (about $40 to

$50 labor), and might be less scary if you are new to this process.

If you take the computer to a shop for repartitioning, be very clear to tell the technician to repartition without erasing your data. This is definitely possible – if the technician says that cannot be done, or if he/she says that you must wipe the hard drive and reinstall all the operating system and programs to that, then take it to another shop. I frequently repartition hard drives without disturbing the data or programs.

I will repeat this warning, for emphasis:

Be sure to read the following chapters on applying this process in various situations before actually proceeding with this. There are some major footnotes, particularly when applying to anything other than a new machine.

Chapter 11 –

How to Do Imaging

There are many software packages on the marketplace which perform the imaging or cloning functions we have described, with similar screen flows. We use as illustration in the following a package called True Image, from www. acronis.com. The screen prints here are from release 8 of that package. Actual screens may be different for the version you use.

> Keep in mind that you will have to translate the drive letter assignments and partition names on these screens to relate those screens to your specific machine.

That is, what is called "WIN_XP" on this screen sequence may be called something else on your machine, and the alternate drive may be assigned a different letter on your machine.

> The process for imaging a partition on a hard drive is this:
>
> 1. Tell the system which partition you wish to image
>
> 2. Tell the system where you wish to put the file which will contain that image
>
> 3. Tell the system what that file will be named

When you first bring up the software, you will see this screen:

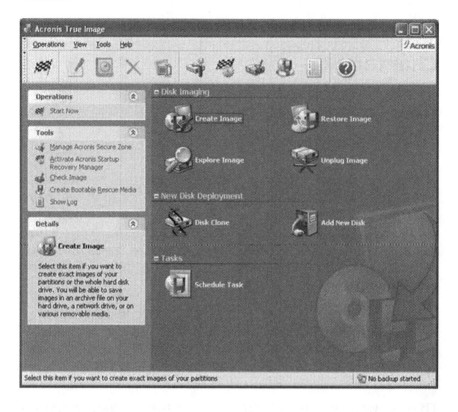

Clicking on Create Image gives you the following sequence:

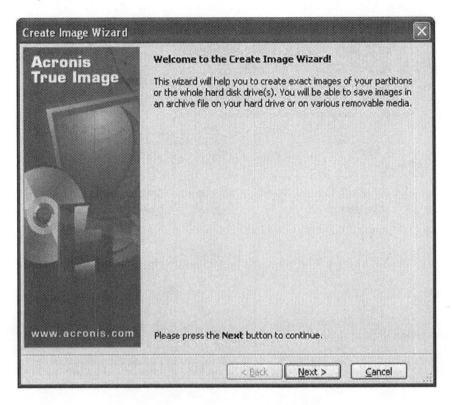

First we have to tell the system which partition we wish to image. In this case, we are selecting the C: drive:

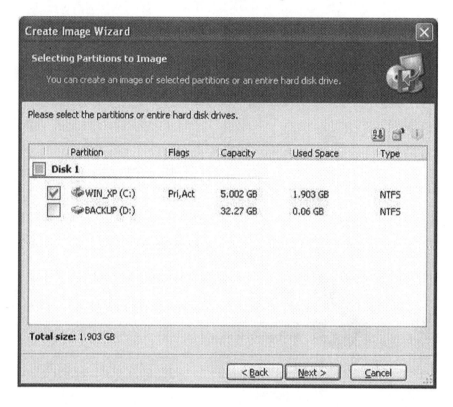

Now we must tell the system where we wish to place that image file after we have created it. In this case, we are selecting as a destination the D: partition which is named "BACKUP" (recall that these letter assignments and names are arbitrary, and may be different on your machine). We created this D: partition in the above step.

We have then selected a Folder in that partition called "Images". Creating a folder for storing your images is a useful tool, so that you can quickly find them later:

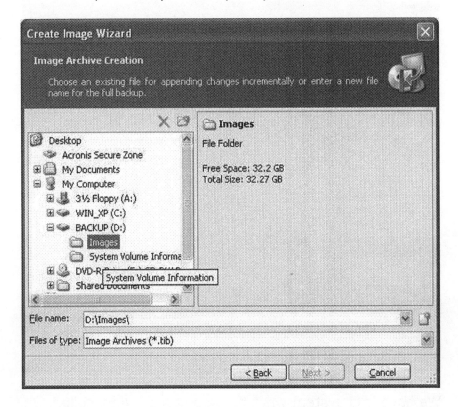

Having selected a place to put that image of the C: drive, we now give it a name:

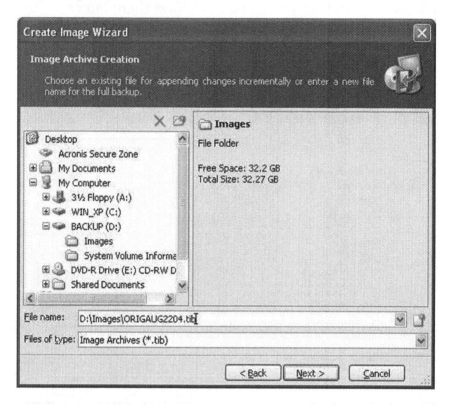

We have told system what the image file will be called. In this case, we have told the system to call the file

ORIGAUG2204.tib

I recommend that you adopt and stick with a rigorous naming convention so that you can later tell what the files are just from their name. You will over time create several of these images.

The "ORIG" part of this file name is my convention for saying "this is the original configuration, before any application software is installed". Thus I know that bringing back this image will restore my system to "out of the box" factory condition. I will create other images later after I install my application software.

The date (August 22 2004) is important: you may later choose to restore an image for a particular date, after you have become used to the process.

The "tib" portion of the file name is used by this particular piece of software as its default file extension. Other imaging programs will use different extensions.

On the next screen we have selected the Full Image backup. It is possible to create "incremental" images, but my recommendation is to always use the full backup option:

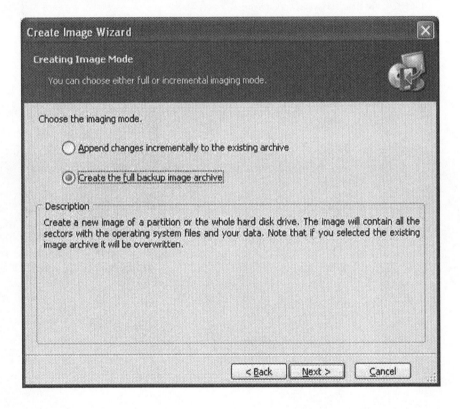

On the next screen I select the Automatic sizing here:

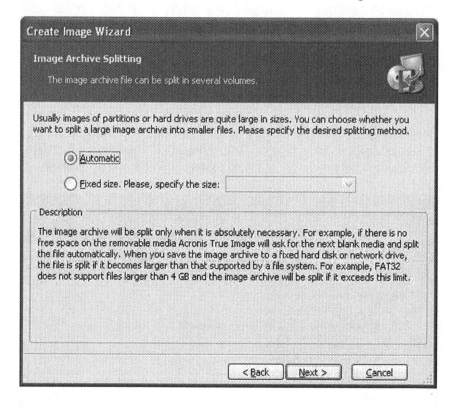

When imaging software creates an image of a partition, it can "compress" the image, permitting it to occupy less physical space in the file created:

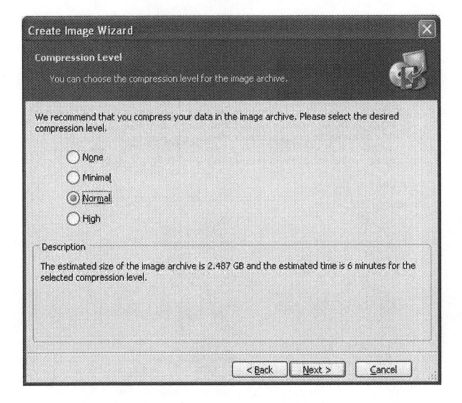

It is possible with this software to password-protect the image file, and if you desire to do that enter the password here:

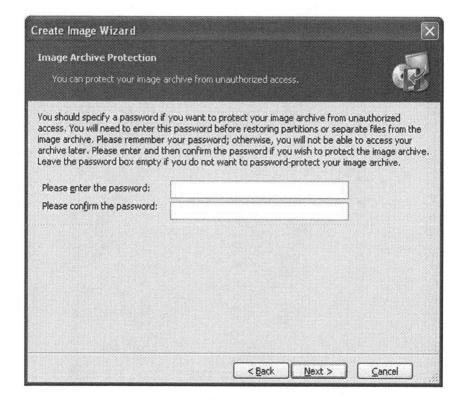

62

There is usually a screen allowing you to place "comments" on the image file, so that later you will know some amount of detail about what is in that file, as in this example where I say what I have done to the machine prior to making the image:

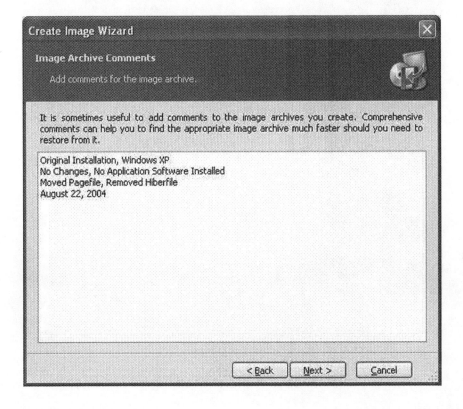

We now get a summary screen showing what we are about to do:

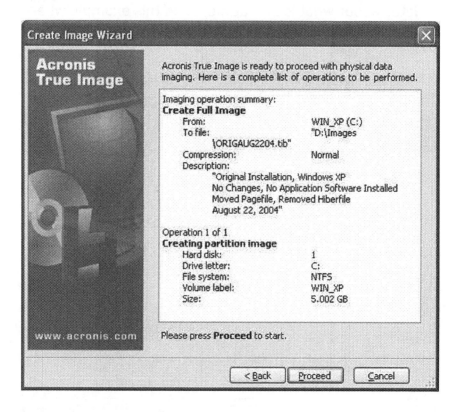

Clicking on Proceed begins the process, and copies the entire C: drive (in this case) to a file containing the image.

A progress screen shows the progress as the image is created, and there is the usual screen indicating process completion:

To restore an image file is exactly the same but in reverse.

The process for restoring an image file is the following:

1. Specify an image file to use in the restore

2. Specify which partition to copy this file onto

The starting screen is the same:

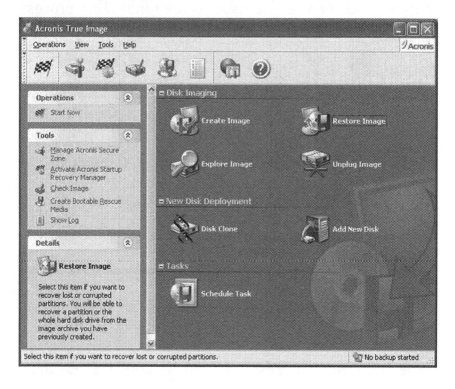

Clicking on Restore Image gives us a wizard as before, and we first select the image file to be used for restoration by browsing on the left side. Once we browse to and click on that image file, the system shows us the comments we inserted when we made that file, so that we can be sure we are restoring the proper one:

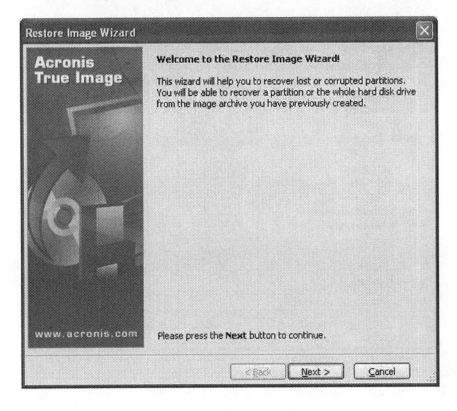

We now browse to find the image file which we wish to restore. In this case, we browse to the D: partition (BACKUP) and select an image file we created at some previous point in time (in this case in the folder Images):

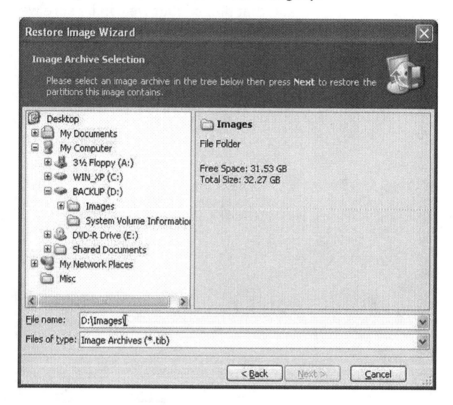

and then:

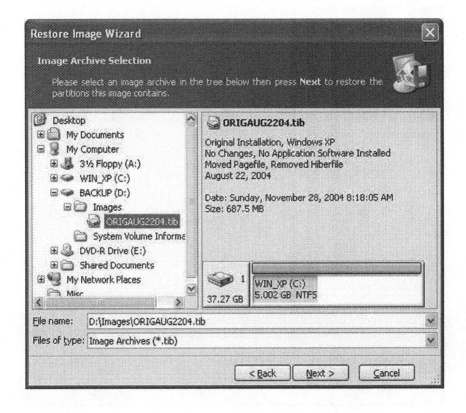

The next screens asks us to tell which partition will be restored using this file. I have selected (and highlighted) the C: drive in this example:

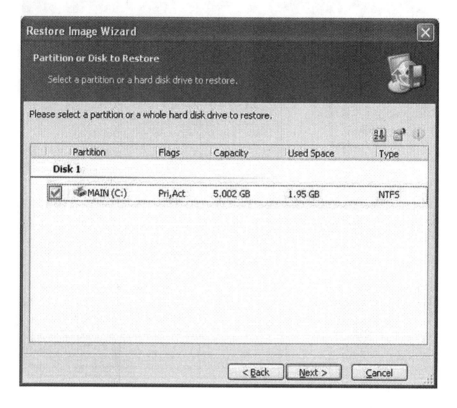

and then:

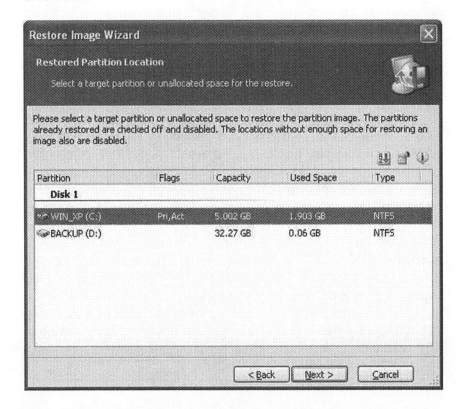

Clicking "Next" begins the process after a warning screen noting that everything on the C: partition will be destroyed. This is normal. If you have never done this before, it will frankly be quite scary the first time you do it – we are destroying the C: drive! However, after the first time it will be routine. It is ok to destroy the entire contents of the C: drive, as we are restoring an exact image of that C: drive from some earlier point in time.

Discussion:

The various software vendors who produce this type of software have slightly different screen paths through this sequence, but the basic process is the same.

There are some notes on this process:

1.   We have illustrated only the basic functions of this software suite – there are a variety of advanced functions which you may use to your advantage after you have mastered the basics, or if you have special requirements. As our target here is the small office user, we are focusing on the "basic" imaging process.

2. Most imaging software allows you to split the image file into smaller pieces, so that you can put the image on CDs or other media for backup purposes. A typical image file of a partition will be at least two to three gigabytes in size after compression, and this is too large to place on one writable CD.

However, I recommend a simpler process. Obtain a DVD burner for your machine and use that to store your image file. A DVD can hold something over 4.5 Gigabytes of data, typically more than enough to hold a compressed partition image if you have adopted our recommendations on keeping the working drive small and manageable. This is simpler, and well worth the expenditure.

3. Disaster Recovery vs. Our Process

Several of the vendors of imaging or cloning software sell their products with a "Backup" or "Disaster Recovery" focus in their advertising.

It is true that disasters happen, such as hard drive total failure. However, these are frankly rare. I personally have never had a hard drive failure, although my father had such a failure recently. It does happen.

However, recovery from a major disaster is not our primary intent here. Our goal is continuing, ongoing, daily perfect operation, with a routine approach that allows you to frequently bring your machine "back to perfect."

Note the difference in emphasis. We are focusing on dealing with the routine, everyday degradation and unpredictable failures that happen on every machine during routine use, not the ability to recover in the event of an extreme and unlikely major disaster. If our Process is applied, then you will certainly have the ability to recover from major disaster in the unlikely case where that happens: you will have an image of your working drive on a DVD and backups of your User Data on CDs or DVDs. However, the approach and thought process we are recommending is much more powerful than this, giving you the ability to focus every day on the work you are trying to perform.

As an example, some software packages of this type give you the ability to perform routine backup images on a schedule, say every Friday night. This is great if your focus is disaster recovery – if you have a major failure you can recover quickly to last Friday. However, what you are doing is imaging a computer which is undergoing normal degradation over time due to normal use, and you are thus recording that constant degradation. It does nothing to maintain your computer in a perfect state. We think there is a better way.

4. Using the "Rescue CDs"

Both of these Acronis packages have the following very nice characteristic: during installation of the software they allow you to create a bootable "Rescue" CD for the software. By booting with this CD in the drive, you will see almost exactly the same screen flow, and can perform all of the functions outside of Windows.

I *STRONGLY* recommend that you do ALL partitioning and imaging functions using these rescue CDs, outside of Windows. This guarantees that you are imaging exactly the installation as you set it up, with no changes occurring as you are performing the imaging. It is possible to do the imaging within Windows, with Windows running, but I do not like this approach. Performing these functions with Windows running is called "hot" imaging, and is intended to let you get work done while the image is being created. However, the time required to make an image is small, is done infrequently, and I recommend the cleaner process of performing the imaging outside of Windows. This avoids all kinds of potential confusions and problems which are too lengthy and complicated to be within the scope of this book.

Chapter 12 –

How to Find and Move the User Files

Recall that the three basic elements of the process are:

1. Build an alternate partition on your hard drive to store all variable information, specifically the User Files and drive images

2. Separate the Program Files from the User Files, putting the Program Files and all stable information on the working Windows partition, typically the C: drive, and putting all the User Files on the alternate partition.

3. Make an image of the Windows partition (typically the C: drive)

We will here do a detailed discussion of exactly how to identify, find, and move the User Files for various types of application programs, with two purposes:

1. To enable you to find and move those files to perform our process

2. If you have a machine which has been in use for some period of time, to enable you to find and back up those files prior to doing some of the operations. This is necessary for several reasons which we will lay out in Chapter 13.

The process is this:

1. For each type of User File create a new folder in your alternate drive to store that type of User File.

2. Move your existing User Files for that application to the new alternate folder

3. As you use each program, use the File-Open and File-Save As functions to save your User Files into that alternate folder and to open files from that folder.

We start with the most commonly used software application: Microsoft Office.

Applying the Process to Microsoft Office

As described above, the goal is to separate the User Files from the Program Files, so that we can routinely image and restore the working drive without erasing any recent work on the User Files. We will move the User Data from its normal place (typically on the C: drive) to an alternate drive.

There are thousands of software application packages in existence. It would be physically impossible to give specific directions (with screen prints) for moving the user files for even a small fraction of these packages.

Therefore, what we will do first is illustrate the process for the most commonly used application package: Microsoft Office. We will then offer suggestions on the typical patterns you will encounter in other software, so that you can successfully move the User Data in other situations.

It turns out that there is a quick and easy way to move the files and documents associated with Microsoft Word, Excel, Powerpoint, and Publisher, all at one time. Unfortunately, this does not affect Outlook and Outlook Express, which are described in the next sections.

Find the "My Documents" folder. It might be on your desktop. If not, click on the Start Button, and look for My Documents. If you do not see My Documents there, then right-click on My Computer and select Explore. You will then see My Documents.

Having found My Documents, right-click on that and select Properties. You will see this screen:

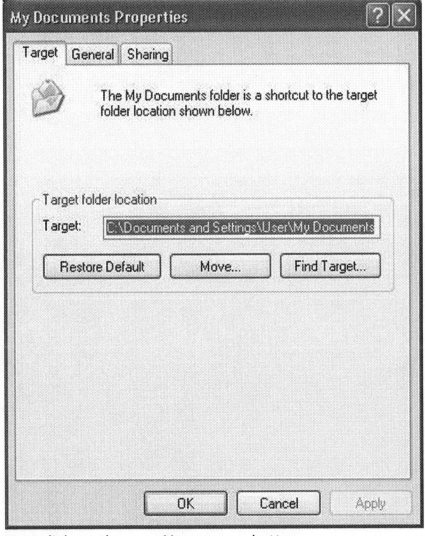

Now click on the   Move...   button.

Assuming that you have previously created a folder on, say, the E: drive called NewLocation, either browse to that folder or type that folder location into the field called Target.

You will then see this screen:

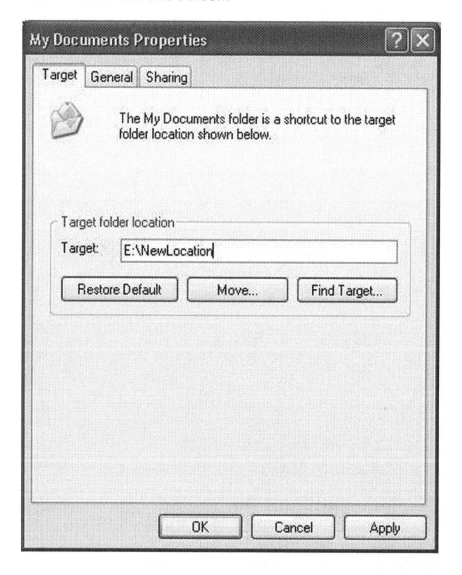

Now Click Apply, and you will see this screen:

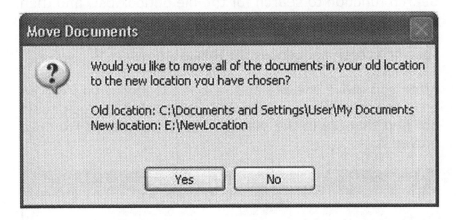

This is a nice touch. The system now asks if you would like to move all of the documents in the old location to the new location. Click on Yes. If you now check any of the Microsoft Office products (typically under Tools-Options in the office application) you will see that the default directory is now E:\NewLocation, and you will find that all of your Office documents are now there.

This is an easy way to move the User Files for Microsoft Word, Microsoft Excel, Microsoft Publisher, and Microsoft Powerpoint in one operation.

Microsoft Outlook

Moving the User Files in Microsoft Outlook is a relatively simple process also.

The user information is kept in a file called outlook.pst.

In a word, all you have to do is physically move that one file, and then re-open Outlook.

Before starting, create a new folder on your Alternate Drive for storing your outlook User Data.

The simplest way to find this file is to use the Windows XP Search function to search for the file outlook.pst, and then to move it to a newly-created folder on your Alternate Drive where you are keeping all of your User Files. We show specific screen sequences for this in Appendix 5.

After you move the file and re-open Outlook, you will an error message like the following, saying that Outlook could not find that file in the place it was expected, as we have moved it:

If you click OK, and get to the main Outlook screen, then click on File-Open-Outlook Data File, and browse to the new location for outlook.pst. The system will then use that newly relocated file for all of its User Data (Inbox, Outbox, Address Book, etc.):

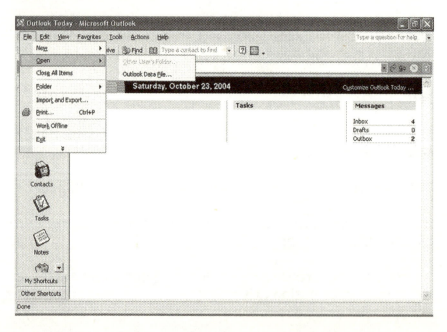

Microsoft Outlook Express

Here is how to move your User Files for Outlook Express.

Before starting, create a new Folder on your alternate drive for Outlook Express to use. In my example, I have created a new folder called OutlookExpressMail on my E: drive.

From the top menu bar, select Tools and then Options:

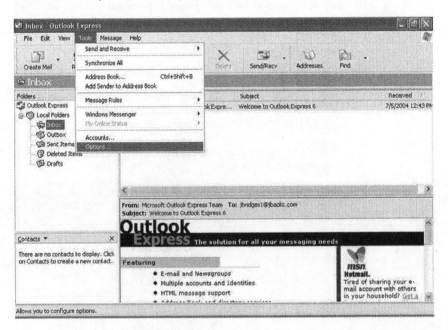

Now click on the Maintenance tab, and then click on the "Store Folder" button:

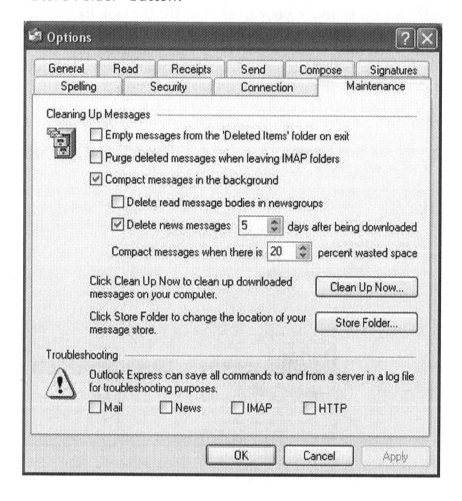

Now click on the "Change" button – we are going to change the location where Outlook Express stores your email information.

Now a browse window will open. It will initially look as follows – you are being shown the present location of your stored User Files for Outlook Express:

Browse to where you have created a new folder for Outlook Express to use. Here we show that I have selected my newly created OutlookExpressMail on my E: drive:

Select OK:

Click on OK.

You will be given the following warning message:

Now close out of Outlook Express.

When you next open Outlook Express, your email files will have moved.

Software with Installation Flexibility

Many modern software vendors anticipate something like this process and provide an option for you when you install the package. One such example is Eudora email, which I personally use.

Prior to installing Eudora, create a directory on your alternate drive to hold your mail files.

If your alternate drive has, say, drive letter E:, then create a folder called, say, Mail on that alternate drive.

Then during the setup of Eudora you will see this sequence of screens:

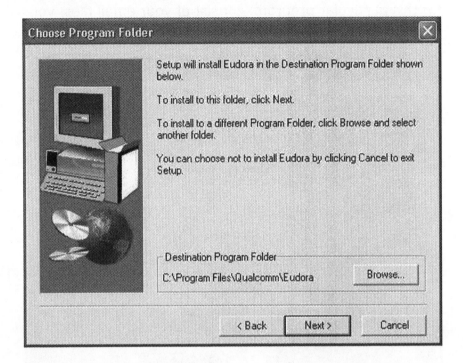

First, Eudora asks you where you want to install the Program Files. You may click Browse and browse to a different location than default if you wish, but there is no particular reason not to take the default.

Then it asks you where you want to store your mail, address books, etc. (what we are calling your User Files). User Files, for this particular program, consist of your email files, your address book, etc. You will see this screen:

Choose Data Folder

Please select the folder where you want Eudora to store mail, settings, address books, etc.:

○ User's Application Data folder.

C:\Documents and Settings\User\Application Data\Qualcomm\Eudora

● Custom Data folder.

Click on the browse button below to select a different folder. The default Data folder for this option is the Destination Program Folder you selected in the previous step.

C:\Program Files\Qualcomm\Eudora   Browse...

< Back   Next >   Cancel

Select the "Custom Data Folder" option. Clicking on Browse produces this screen:

Click on the down arrow at the bottom (drives), select your alternate drive as depicted here:

Highlight your newly created Mail folder and click OK, producing this screen, acknowledging the change:

The next screen verifies all of these choices:

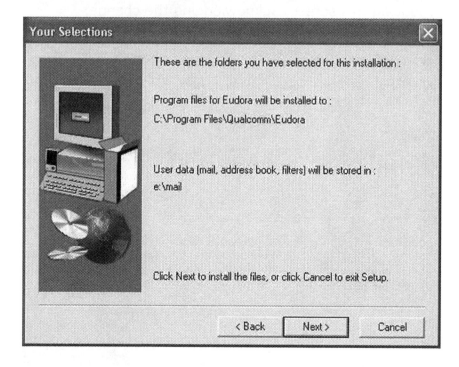

You are on your way.

Other Software Applications

In most cases, finding the user files is straightforward because the User Files are easily identifiable.

All Windows files have the format:

xxx.yyy

where

1.   the "xxx" is the file name, and

2.   the "yyy" designates the type of the file.   This is called an "extension".

All Microsoft Word documents, for example, have the form

xxx.doc

where the "xxx" is the file name, and the ".doc" extension identifies the file as a Microsoft Word document.

Thus, a letter created in Microsoft Word might have a file name of

Letter to Joe.doc

Similarly, all Microsoft Excel spreadsheets have the extension of ".xls" on the end.

A Microsoft Excel spreadsheet, then, may have a name such as

February Business Plan Forecast.xls

and a Quickbooks file might have a name such as

XYZ Incorporated.qbw

with the "xls" and "qbw" file extensions telling us what type of file they are.

If you are confused about what the default file extension is, in most programs you can do the following:

1. Open the program

2. Create a dummy document or other user file

3. Click on File-Save As

You will get a picture similar to the following:

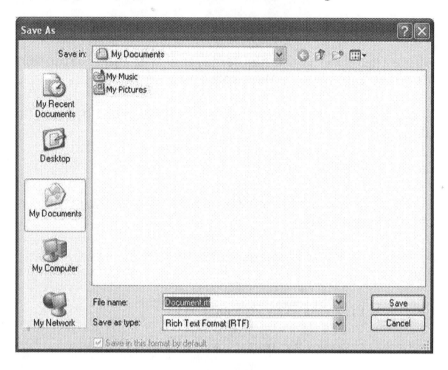

This particular example is from Wordpad, which is a simple word processing utility on all Windows machines.

Note the line at the bottom: When you do a File-Save As in any program, the line at the bottom tells you the default that the program will use. There are often other options but the default shows first. In this particular case, unless you change it, the file type will be ".rtf", standing for (as shown in the window) Rich Text Format.

Similarly, saving a document in Microsoft Word will show a default of ".doc", and saving a spreadsheet in Microsoft Excel will show a default of ".xls".

In the case illustrated, we now know that we are looking for files with ".rtf" as the extension.

Unless specific instructions are given above (e.g., for Microsoft Office), the general process for moving your User Files for each of your application programs is:

a) Identify the User Files

b) Create a folder on your alternate partition to hold those User Files

c) Find the User Files

d) Move the User Files

To repeat, if any of these tasks (finding files, creating folders, moving files) is unfamiliar to you, please read and study the Windows Primer in Appendix 5.

Final Note on User Files:

Although most application packages have clearly-identifiable User Files which can be located and moved, there are exceptions, the most common exception being America Online. For an example, and for instructions on how to deal with these applications, please read Appendix 4.

Chapter 13 -

Evaluating Your Computing Environment Before Starting

We will describe various computer hardware and working arrangements, and will lay out the process for each case.

In order to avoid repetition, the following notes apply to all of the cases:

1. DVD Burner

Have a combination DVD burner/CD burner installed on your machine if it does not already have one. This will make your life much easier. The DVD burner can also burn CDs, so that when backing up your files you can use CDs for the smaller user files and the DVDs for larger ones. A DVD can hold 4.6 gigabytes of data, a huge benefit if you are backing up large user files.

You can also copy your image files onto a DVD after you create them. If you have reduced the size of your working drive properly, this should easily hold that image, especially after compression.

2. Backing up and removing files

If you are starting with anything other than a new machine, we will tell you to back up and <u>remove</u> your user data files from the hard drive prior to performing this process, for two reasons:

a) To make the working drive (generally the C: drive) as small as possible for imaging

b) To allow for recovery if anything goes wrong.

This is a standard procedure in any machine rearrangement. If you are unsure about which files to back up, please read the above chapter on User Files. That describes how to identify the user files for various types of applications. You may then use either built-in backup functions in each application or use the Windows Search function to find the files needing to be backed up, and then use standard Windows functions to write to a CD or the software that comes with your DVD burner to write to that medium.

Whenever backing up for this kind of machine rearrangement, be very sure that you have backed up everything on the machine that you might ever need. Do not forget address books, mailing lists, and favorites if those are important to you. Go through your Add/Remove program list and every icon on your desktop and think about each application – are there files associated with this application which I will need later? Do not forget Outlook or Outlook Express.

Note: If you have been operating in a "TV set" mode (see Chapter 3) for some time, and have never backed up your data, this will admittedly be a painful process the first time. You will have to figure out what files to back up, locate them, and move them to a backup medium. Although it is painful, you are at serious risk anyway if you don't do this. Should you have a hardware failure, or should a virus or worm sneak by your defenses, you are at risk of losing all of your data anyway. Taking the time to do this and to apply the process we are describing will allow you to not only operate in a perfect mode every day, but will facilitate recovery in the event one of these things happens.

3. Other Useful Software Utilities

I found that certain utilities are very useful for maintaining perfect operation. These are not strictly necessary, but I have found them useful. These are:

a) Internet Cleanup Software

This software cleans your machine of history lists, temporary internet files, and many other types of junk files. There are many good brands on the marketplace.

Just prior to making a disk image, I run my cleanup software, to make sure I am not imaging unnecessary temporary or other junk files, thus making sure my image is as clean as possible.

b) Disk Wiping Software

This software wipes the file slack space in between files, wipes free space, cleans out old entries from directories, etc. Just because you have erased a file on your machine does not mean that it is gone. Windows simply marks the directory entry as "erased", but the file is still there and may be seen by appropriately skilled individuals. This software physically wipes these files and other spare space on your hard drive. In addition to privacy and safety, wiping in this manner makes the compression performed by the imaging software more efficient in many cases, and generally contributes to a clean imaging process.

c) Spyware Removal Software

Although strictly not necessary (the imaging process insures that no spyware remains on your machine after an image is restored), I use two packages to guarantee that I have kept the machine in as perfect a condition as possible.

Two good free programs are Adaware (www.lavasoft.com) and Spybot Search & Destroy (www.safer-networking.org). Be sure to get the right ones – many spyware programs are deceptively named to take advantage of these individuals' good reputations. Microsoft recently released its anti-spyware Beta.

Four Situations

We approach four cases which you might have as you consider applying this process:

1. You are willing to buy a new computer to start this process, so that you can start with a pure working environment. This is the ideal situation.

If that is the case, then we describe in Appendix 1 my personal recommendations for the type of new computer to buy. There are also recommendations in Appendices 2 and 3 on how to set up a new machine.

2. You have a reasonably modern computer and can bring the machine back to original brand-new condition.

3. You have a reasonably modern computer, but for some reason cannot bring the machine back to original brand-new condition.

4. You have an older computer.

A Brand New Machine

In Appendix 1 we describe our recommendations for the ideal new machine. Assuming that you are willing and able to do that, then follow the directions in the following section beginning at Step 3. If you have the machine built with the hard drive already partitioned, you may start at Step 4.

A Modern Machine, Restored to Original Condition

This chapter would apply if you have a reasonably modern machine (say less than two or three years old) running Windows XP, and you have the ability to restore the machine to an original installation condition.

(Terminology: a "white box" machine is a machine custom built for you by a reputable local computer shop. They generally come in white or beige boxes, thus the name. This is in contrast to "mass-produced" machines from such vendors as Dell, Compaq, Gateway, Hewlett-Packard, etc., and of course laptops.)

There are generally two situations:

a. You have a mass-produced machine with a restore CD (or a restore function) which can bring the machine to original factory condition, or have a brand-new mass-produced computer. This would include, for example, a new laptop.

b. You have a white box machine built by a local computer shop with the original Windows XP CD, drivers CDs, and application CDs available, so that you can physically re-install the operating system and all applications, erasing all of the old programs and data.

For simplicity, we will refer to both of these situations as "original factory condition".

That is, you have a machine situation where it is possible to take the machine back to its original pure form, and you are willing to do so. This is often not possible (see the next section).

Steps to follow:

1. Use your DVD/CD burner to back up all of your user data files, and remove them from the machine completely.

See the discussion above on identifying the User Files, and see the Windows Primer for directions on physically moving these files to your backup medium.

After you restore your machine back to original factory condition, all of your user data will be gone. Therefore, be very sure of these backups.

2. After you have backed up all of your user files and verified and re-verified that you have everything you need off of that hard drive, restore your machine to original, brand-new condition:

a) If you have a white box machine, re-install the Windows XP operating system, erasing everything on the C: drive, and then re-install the drivers that came with your machine.

b) If you have a mass produced machine, apply the restore function provided by the manufacturer to bring the machine back to original factory condition. In some cases this will be done by a CD or DVD provided by the manufacturer, and in other cases it is an option you see during boot-up, with the restore files physically on the hard drive itself in a "hidden" partition.

In either case, after applying this restore, you will have a machine in its original brand-new or factory-delivered condition.

3. Either take your machine to a local computer shop and have them repartition the hard drive into a C: drive with 5 gigabytes of space and a D: drive with all other space, or do the repartitioning yourself (see Chapter 10).

4. Having restored your machine to original condition and having divided the hard drive into at least two partitions:

a) Set up your internet connection

b)   Activate your installation of Windows XP if necessary (<u>very important</u> – if you do not do this, your archived image will be useless later!)

c)   Go to the Windows Update site and do all necessary Windows Updates, for security reasons

d)   Make an immediate image of the C: drive (or primary working partition) and call it something like "ORIGDATE.???." The "ORIG" portion of the file name indicates that this is the pure original installation, with no changes. The "???" here is a result of the fact that different imaging software will produce files with different file extensions. The "DATE" portion of the file name should be something like February 5 2004, so that later you can tell when this original image was made.

The resulting file name might be something like

ORIGNov182004.tib

with the "ORIG" indicating that this is the original, raw installation, and the date.

e) Copy this image onto a writable DVD for safety. You can always bring your machine back to this perfect original state quickly by restoring that image from the DVD.

f)   Install (or re-install) your various Applications – word processing, spreadsheet, email, etc.

g) For each application you intend to use, arrange so that the User Data files are physically moved to your alternate drive.

h) Verify and re-verify that the user files created by each application are physically on your alternate drive. Do this by creating dummy files in each application and verifying using the Windows Search function that when they are saved they are physically on your alternate drive, not your primary working drive.

i) For mass-produced machines, I recommend that you remove unnecessary application packages. These can be found in the Add/Remove Programs section (Start-Settings-Control Panel-Add/Remove Programs). These would typically include organizer, music, photo manager, greeting card maker, and other "fluff" software, and games. Photo manager software in particular is a space hog.

j) Now make another image of your C: drive (or primary working partition) and put that image on a DVD also.

The image file name might be something like:

CNov152004.tib

with the "C" indicating that it is a backup of the C: drive, and the date indicating the obvious. You can then tell from the file name itself some basic information about the image.

You now have two image files on hand:

a) An image of the pure original installation, fresh "from the box". You can always come back to this installation if necessary.

b) An image of the original installation with all of your application software packages installed fresh. This is a good initial restore point in most situations, with recovery back to "original factory" available as a backup.

A Modern Machine, Not Restorable to Original Condition

The above is all well and good if you have a brand new machine and can start out clean, or if you have original installation CDs where you can bring your machine back to it's original pure out-of-the-box state. However, that is sometimes not possible.

Frankly, it is highly recommended that you do exactly that if there is any way possible.

However, this may be impractical or impossible for a variety of reasons. For example, you may have lost the recovery CDs for your machine.

How Full Is Your Hard Drive?

If you cannot, for whatever reason, take your machine back to original condition, then this question becomes the dominant factor - how full is your hard drive?

Our goal is to create a relatively small working C: drive and partition the hard drive with a larger D: drive (letters may be different of course) containing all the user data and larger files.

> You cannot create a new partition on a hard drive unless there exists on that hard drive an appropriate amount of free space for that new partition.

In order to create a new 30 gigabyte alternate partition on the hard drive you must have 30 gigabytes of unused space on the hard drive. As an obvious and extreme example, if your machine has a 40 gigabyte hard drive and you have 38 gigabytes full of programs and data, you cannot proceed.

There is some common sense required here.

You must, therefore, use your DVD burner (see above) to back up and remove from the hard drive all of your user files and large data files prior to doing this process, just as in the situation above. I would recommend that you remove files until the entire used portion of the hard drive is less than 5 gigabytes. Unless you have a rare situation, this should be possible. At any rate, remove everything possible from the hard drive – the goal is to make the working Windows drive as small as possible.

Having removed all of your user files from the machine, and reduced the size of the working C: drive, then do a re-partitioning of the hard drive or have that done for you, as described above.

The process then is as follows:

a) First, make sure everything works. If there is any known problem, then pay a computer shop if necessary to fix the problem.   If you have extraneous toolbars that have installed themselves on your Internet Explorer, or if any program doesn't work quite correctly, pay someone if necessary to correct the situation.

We are going to split and image the hard drive, so that whatever does not work now will also not work in the future. This is why the wipe and re-install sequence is so strongly recommended - the existing system may have hidden degradation and problems you don't know about, but which will cause problems later.   There is no way to know, no matter how careful you are.

b) Buy a cleanup utility (see above) and clean all of the temporary, history, and other junk off of your machine.

c) Buy a wiping utility, and wipe the slack and spare space in your hard drive thoroughly.   This will insure that the data on the hard drive which you think is erased is actually erased, that directories are cleaned of names which no longer exist, and so on. We want our original setup to be as pure as possible, given that we are starting with a machine corrupted to some degree.

d) Obtain a good virus scanning software package, and run a thorough virus scan on your hard drive, being sure to use the current virus definitions.

e) Obtain a good spyware/adware cleanup utility program, and have this program clean all malware off of your hard drive. (See above)

f) Defragment your drive, cleanup and wipe again.

g) Partition your hard drive into a working C: partition of approximately 5 gigabytes and with a D: partition containing all of the rest of the space (see discussion above).

h) Make an immediate image copy of the C: drive. You now have your entire C: drive imaged in its present form.

i) Now modify all your programs so that the user files are on the alternate drive, not on the primary working drive, as described above.

j) Make a new image of the C drive and a backup of the essential files now living on the D drive.

You have an Older Machine

This would apply if your machine is more than, say, 3 years old or if you are still running Windows 98 or (heaven forbid) Windows 95.

Frankly, I recommend buying a new machine.

Modern imaging software may or may not work on your older machine, and there may be hardware or other incompatibilities. I have several machines which I use for testing, and the one of the most commonly-used and best-known imaging software packages failed on one of my older machines, with indecipherable error messages which the vendor could not resolve even with several emails back and forth with what I would call quite competent technical support. Even reputable and competent vendors cannot allow for every old hardware situation – there are just too many variables. Asking modern software vendors to backwards-adapt to all old types of hardware and operating environments is unrealistic.

If money is tight, then you may buy a new machine with more-than-adequate horsepower from one of the mass manufacturers for under $400, and after paying a computer shop to add a DVD burner and do the partitioning, you have a brand-new machine for under $550 which, after applying our process, will last you indefinitely in perfect working order.

Appropriate for all cases: Please see Appendices 2 and 3 with my recommendations for setting up your machine.

Chapter 14 – Ongoing Changes

Assume that you have partitioned the drive, set up your applications so that the User Data is physically on your alternate partition, and made a perfect image copy of your C drive. You use the computer for a while, restoring as necessary to bring the machine back to good form.

Now, some change occurs:

> You get a new version of your accounting software

> Microsoft comes out with a service pack you need to install

> You decide to change your email software

> You buy an upgrade to your FTP software

> You obtain a new application package that you need to use for some function.

That is, something has happened which affects your actual programs on the C: drive.

Here's what I do:

1. Restore my last drive image, to make sure I am starting with a pure system.

2. Install the microsoft patch, software update, or whatever is new that is needed.

3. Defrag, wipe, clean.

4.   Make a new drive image with a new date.

By starting this update process with a pure drive image, you guarantee that any new drive images are pure, uncorrupted by any recent use of your computer.

I keep three or four recent historical images of my C: drive available at all times, plus the "original".

You will learn over time by experience when to make new images.

Chapter 15 – Backing up

Everyone knows that we should backup data.

But do you do it?

I have the usual horror stories of friends of mine who didn't back up, and who are now religious about it after some disaster occurred. The problem is, in a typical installation, with everything living on the C: drive, exactly what do you back up?

Some programs have a backup function in the software, and some don't. The problem is that in general it is difficult to answer the following series of questions:

a)   What exactly do I back up?

b)   Which files? Which files are real user data, and which ones are application files?

c)   Where are they? User data lives in a variety of directories for the different software applications, often two and three levels deep. The User Files for Outlook Express are five levels deep in the directory tree.

d)   How specifically do I restore these files if and when I ever need them?

This last is extremely important. Even if you do back up your data, how precisely do you restore those backup files after an emergency? Exactly which files do you bring back and where do you put them? This is often not straightforward.

Even with programs like my Quickbooks accounting software, which has built-in backup functions, if you are an accountant handling many customers with Quickbooks, opening each customer in Quickbooks and backing up their data is a very time-consuming process.

If you back up entire folders (to be safe) you end up with huge backup files, and restoring after a disaster is not straightforward.   Usually it's not clear exactly which files you need or how to bring them back.   Therefore, serious backing up can be a painful and lengthy process, so we tend to avoid it.

At least I used to.

But note the difference now.   Since we have moved all the data over onto an alternate partition, I can now burn CDs with backup data simply and quickly, by just archiving the data files now on D: (or other drive letter, as the case may be).   These files are now conveniently located in one place.

Here is what the alternate drive (where I have all of my business User Files) looks like on my machine:

The right side of the screen shows the folders containing my User Data. I have modified this somewhat for illustration purposes, but notice that I have all my user data in one clear, easily-accessible place. I simply drag each folder over to the H: drive (my CD burner), and do a burn with the built-in XP CD burn function. It literally takes less than five minutes. Having done the setup work we are recommending, there is no confusion whatsoever about what to backup.

As this method makes backups easy, *I actually do it more often*.

Therefore, even if a future virus manages to corrupt drives other than the C: drive or does other major damage to your hard drive (assuming such a virus can get by your anti-virus software), or if your hard drive fails completely (a rare occurrence but one which does happen), a side effect of this process is to make backing up data very easy and quick, so that I will actually do it more often and thus have backups on hand, minimizing the damage even in these unlikely cases.

Very simply, a virus cannot get into your desk drawer.

Chapter 16 –

The Process in Practice

Note the advantage of the image arrangement described above. If a program or function simply stops working for no reason, or if a spyware hacker gets into my machine, or if my child accidentally messes something up or installs a cool malware-laden cursor, I simply restore a drive image, and move on. This takes a few minutes, and the problem is eliminated. I do not have to go through complex virus-removal processes, with registry changes, downloaded virus removal software, etc. I just bring back a pure copy of the C: drive and move on. It takes me literally five minutes.

When SearchBar and Bargain Buddy appeared, I just did an image restore and went back to work. I suppose I ought to have checked out the Free $$$ before I restored..... hmmmmmm. I wonder how much "free" money I lost out on... .

Freedom

Note another side aspect to doing things this way, other than avoiding danger and degradation - I am completely free to use my computer for any purpose whatsoever and in any way whatsoever with zero worry. I can always, no matter what, bring it back to perfect in a few minutes, absolutely no matter what happens.

Suppose, for example, that I wish to try some shareware or other utility to help me with some job.

This is a real example. I was doing internet research on a certain topic for a volunteer group that I belong to. Because I was looking at many web pages and wanted to save certain ones for future reference, I looked around for a "bookmark manager" piece of software, to help with that task. There are many available.

In the prior world, I would have the following gamble: I can try various shareware or utility programs, and gamble. All software looks good in the writeup, and all websites brag about how wonderful their software is. I can download something I'd like to try, install it, and see what happens.

Suppose it not only is no good but causes all kinds of problems. In the old world, I'm stuck. Uninstalls rarely work well, and my machine is forever degraded. Or I might try three or four utilities before I find one that I like, uninstall the others, and hope (good luck!) that the uninstalls actually worked and left no damage.

This is a heck of a gamble if my machine is important to me.

In my present world, I am free to try and look at anything whatsoever, with complete peace of mind. Once I've looked over various utilities, I bring back the last drive image, knowing I have a pure install, and move on. There is zero risk.

During the preparation of this manuscript, I decided to send a draft to a friend of mine who did not have Microsoft Word but who did have Adobe Acrobat. Therefore, I looked for Word-to-PDF conversion software, as I had not done this before.

I did a Google search, found an interesting-looking candidate, and downloaded and installed the Demonstration version. When I ran it, I got a message saying "This package does not work with the free version of Acrobat Reader".

No problem. Except when I clicked out of the message, I got Windows exception error messages – it didn't stop cleanly.

Not to worry, let's try another package. I now downloaded and installed the demonstration version of the second good-looking candidate from the Google search. This seemed to install well, but when I opened my document (with the intent to convert to pdf format) I got an error – there were macros in the new software, and I had not enabled macros when I initially installed my Microsoft Word. Word was now allowing me to open my documents only in read-only mode.

I growled briefly, and decided that I had better do more research and get some advice before I tested any more packages.

In the old world, I would uninstall these two packages and hope that no damage was done to my computer.

In my present world, I do my five-minute restore sequence, and have complete peace of mind that my machine is in exactly the same condition as before I tried those two pieces of software. This freedom and peace of mind is priceless.

As I was finishing up an edit of this book, the following happened.

I was testing a particular antivirus and firewall combination. During the testing, I suddenly got a Windows error saying that an illegal access had been attempted.

Immediately the anti-virus software popped up a bright orange screen that a certain bad piece of software had been detected, and it then notified me that notepad.exe had been removed, as it had been infected. Great, the antivirus software was on the job. Except now notepad is gone. Hmmm....do I want to take the time to get that back? How do I do that? Does it matter? I don't know.......hmmmm.

Some users might even ask "what is Notepad anyway?" A reasonable question for many people. It might be important and might not be. How are you to know? And how would you get it back?

Doesn't matter.

This was a test environment, of course, but had it happened on my primary working machine, I would simply do my five-minute restore sequence, and go about my work. I wouldn't waste any time at all worrying about Notepad or the worm. Similarly, in the case where my brother's Front Page stopped working for no apparent reason - if he had had this arrangement in place, he would do his restore and move on. He would not know or care why it stopped working in the first place.

During the preparation of this manuscript the following happened. My brother bought a new laptop just prior to a trip. He networked the laptop into his main machine and brought over several files he needed for the trip. When he finished, he found that, for some very strange and unknown reason, his satellite internet connection (he lives in the back woods) had stopped working. He did not have much time before he had to leave to catch his plane, and there were some things he needed to do. This was a crisis. There simply wasn't time to take the machine to a shop or call a friend for help or wander around the system hoping to find the setting change.

By this time I had shown him this Process and he had installed it on his machine. Rather than spending any time at all worrying about why the satellite connection no longer worked, he just restored an image of his C: drive, and everything was back to perfect again. The problem was instantly solved.

This works. It's a bit scary the first time you try it, but after a while you'll do it without even thinking.

Problem of any kind?

Restore.

Problem gone, back to perfect, back to work.

Chapter 17 –

Some Misconceptions and Questions

The purpose of this part of the book has been to acquaint you with the true nature of the problems computer users face, and to acquaint you with enough conceptual fundamentals to convince you that a solution is possible.

There are some natural questions which might arise in the reader's mind, such as:

> Question: "If I accept what you are saying, namely that I can recover quickly if I get a virus, then is it the case that I do not need anti-virus and firewall software?"

Answer: No.

There are some particularly nasty viruses running around, some of which can destroy your boot sector (which is the first place Windows looks when it is beginning to start up) or can destroy enough of your hard drive to require you to do a complete wipe of the hard drive, reformat, and re-install of all operating systems and programs. True, if you have imaged and backed up in the recommended way, recovery in these extreme situations is easier than it would be otherwise. However, there is no point to volunteering for these problems.

That's like volunteering for a broken leg because you know the doctor can fix it up pretty quickly.

Whichever antivirus and firewall package you select, be sure that the package does automatic updating of its software and tables frequently.

Also, be sure that your firewall package notifies you whenever any program is trying to access the internet. This gives you control if some program sneaks onto your machine and tries to send out spam email without your knowledge. Mcafee notifies me when, for example, I send three or four nearly identical emails to my customers, just in case a worm has gotten into my machine.

Question: "If, as you say, restoring an image makes my machine perfect, getting rid of any spyware or malware which is there, do I need to obtain and run anti-spyware/adware software?"

Answer: In my opinion, yes.

This is a personal opinion. I am a purist, and possibly an extremist when it comes to keeping my machines in absolutely perfect working order. I run Spybot Search & Destroy and Adaware on an occasional basis to make sure that things are still as perfect as I think they are.

You may note that, up above, we suggest that you go back and bring in a pure image before doing any additions, and then making a new image before this has a chance to get corrupted.

Once I got a bit lazy about this. I restored an image one night on my home machine, and early the next afternoon had some change that I needed to make. I thought that there had not been enough time or internet activity for anything bad to happen, so did the change and made an image. Later I discovered that that there were several entries like "xxxpornoxxx" in my registry, that had somehow crept in during this brief time period.

Therefore, it does not hurt to obtain and run these packages on occasion, as there are free versions and they will give you the peace of mind that you have in fact kept everything perfect.

Question: "Why, instead of going to all of this trouble (and rearranging my entire computer), can't I just get good anti-virus, firewall, spyware removal, machine cleanup, and registry cleaning software and run these on a routine basis? Won't these take care of all the problems?"

Answer: Certainly you can approach it this way, and many people do. But here are some thoughts:

1. This approach does not take care of all the unpredictable things that happen to users, such as when something simply fails or stops working for no apparent reason. Some problems and corruptions have nothing to do with spyware or viruses.

2. Cleaning software, such as registry cleaning software, has to walk a fine line. It has to clean clearly inappropriate items, but cannot change too much. The last thing a software builder wants to have happen is to have you run the software and then have the machine fail, giving you the usual incomprehensible error message. Therefore, the builders of such software must of necessity lean on the side of caution: when in doubt, leave it alone. Therefore, of necessity, some things will be left there over time that should not be there.

Cleaning software does not restore your system "back to perfect." It cannot do this because the software does not know what "perfect" was.

3. Cleaning software, such as spyware/adware removal packages, do selected things and only selected things.

For example, the two packages which I use (Spybot Search & Destroy and Adaware) have different lists of spyware to be removed, and neither makes a claim to have every possible piece of spyware in its database. These folks, although very good, can only respond to spyware attacks of which they are aware, and for which they have resources to do the programming.

No vendor can claim to have every possible spyware program in its database, and it would be ridiculous to make such a claim since new threats are being generated literally every day. Therefore, the approach of using this type of software frequently, although good, does not guarantee the perfect operation we are seeking.

As an obvious aside, anti-virus software vendors have an equivalent problem, no matter how competent and reputable they might be – you will never see a reputable anti-virus vendor advertising that they have every single virus in their database.

Yahoo email, for example, automatically scans attachments for viruses. It uses well-known and well-reputed Norton antivirus, and came at the time of this writing with this disclaimer, illustrating the above point:

"Disclaimer: This virus scanner may not be able to detect or repair all viruses and variants. Please be aware that there is a risk involved whenever you download email attachments to your computer or send email attachments to others, and that, as provided in the Terms of Service, neither Yahoo! nor its licensors are responsible for any damages caused by your decision to do so."

This does not at all mean that Norton is incompetent; it merely means that there are practical limitations to what antivirus firms can achieve, as we have pointed out.

4. This brings up another point. How do you know what your "cleaning" software is doing? I mean: what it is doing precisely? All software looks good on the web site, with

great claims about all the good things it is doing and the usual "greatest thing since sliced bread" testimonials.

However, these claims are always in broad marketing terms. Exactly what is being done? Is it doing everything possible? Exactly what is it doing and how? Since these questions are generally not answered specifically, you are gambling that the cleaning software builder is doing a good job. How do you know? You don't. You are trusting someone you have never met to properly do a process you don't understand, and with the details not being revealed.   All you know is that something is happening when the program runs, and you are hoping it is good and that it is good enough.

5.   This brings up yet another point.   Particularly when it comes to spyware removal software, the game on the internet is, unfortunately, "no holds barred".

This means that unscrupulous spyware makers have the audacity to advertise themselves as spyware removal products, when in fact they are installing spyware on your machine. "Free Scan for Spyware" buttons on websites or advertisements may be a simple front for installing spyware. How do you know? You don't. This is much like certain criminal "financial consultants" who take your money not for the purpose of investing it but for the purpose of stealing it.

Again, you are trusting someone you have never met with your business machine and your livelihood.

There is no need to trust anyone – the process we are recommending maintains perfect machine operation at all times.

Chapter 18 -

Conclusion

The astute reader will have noticed that running throughout this entire book is something of a "sales pitch" – I have attempting to sell you a Process for setting up your computer that permits you to take it "back to perfect" anytime you please, for any reason you please.

This is out of line with normal "selling" technique. Normal selling would have the reader (hopefully) agree to the problem statement, after which the discussion changes to the sale of the "solution".

There is a reason for this barrage of examples and continued "selling", based on my experience. Permit me to illustrate with an example:

A friend of mine approached me, desperate for help. Her machine was in bad shape. As it turns out, her machine had been infected with many instances of the adware/ spyware which was discussed above. She had a particularly nasty form of adware on her machine which watched her keystrokes, and fed her popup advertisements based on her typing. Everything was taking forever. Her Quickbooks was taking several minutes to start up, for no apparent reason.

I gave her a draft of this book to read, and she read the first few chapters with great excitement – she could relate big time!

Meanwhile I took a look at her machine, used some adware/spyware removal utilities to get rid of the immediate infection, and did some other simple cleanups. Her Quickbooks now came up quickly, and the machine was temporarily back to "normal."

Whereupon she lost interest in reading the rest of the book.

This is the trap. We tend to muddle through and put up with ever-increasing grief until it gets unbearable, whereupon we find a friendly nerd to help out or hire a computer shop and things get "sort of" back to normal (or even buy a new machine), whereupon we resume the "TV set" operation mode mentioned in Chapter 3. The thought is "was it really that bad?" And the time, energy, and risk involved with setting up a permanent solution seems at that particular point in time an unnecessarily large and risky effort, until of course something else happens.

Muddling along seems good enough most of the time – the computer works most days.

Only when "disaster" happens (e.g., something that simply stops working for no apparent reason and at a particularly bad time) do we then return to panic mode, and try to recover yet again.

The process we are recommending is admittedly a bit scary if you've never tried it before. I know that you will have some raised blood pressure the first time you see a screen that says "we are about to erase the contents of your C: drive", but after you see it actually work just one time, it will be easy.

I will close with two examples.

It is a Saturday, and I am writing this "Conclusion" chapter. My father was trying to type an email. I get a panic call from his wife saying that while typing he got a strange message with something about "keys" (which she couldn't remember) and all of a sudden the keyboard wouldn't work at all!

Fortunately, they had me to call, and after some muddling I pointed her to the Control Panel, and with a setting change things were back to normal. How did this setting get changed, and in the middle of simply typing an email? I have absolutely no idea. An expert might know, but I certainly don't. In fact, the expert might even say "this is impossible", but it happened.

More importantly, what if she had not had me to call? And what if that computer was needed on a Saturday for some urgently needed work?

What if it is a holiday and all computer shops are closed and all your computer-expert friends are out of town? I can tell you from my experience as a small businessman that I do a lot of my work on weekends. What realistically would you do? What if it is a holiday and you have some very important work to send to a customer, that simply must get done right now? What realistically do you do?

As a small businessperson, you have no idea when or where these strange incidents will strike you, and they can have a very large impact on your operation, especially when you need to get something done urgently. If you have set up the process we have detailed, then no matter what happens, you can be back to perfect, guaranteed, without calling anyone, no matter what time of day or night it is. It works.

My last example might be the best example of all of the power of this process.

A week and a half ago (prior to writing this conclusion chapter) something happened to my main machine, along the lines of the examples given in this book. I grumbled a bit, did my restore image process and went back to work. I remember thinking at the time that "this will make an excellent example for my book." However, when I tried to remember what it was a week later in order to write it up, I simply could not remember what happened. I racked my brain, but could not remember.

That is to say, because I have this process established and routinely working, whatever happened became so minor in the effect on my work day and had such a small impact on my life that I simply could not remember for the life of me what it was a week later. Do you remember every gnat that flies across your desk or every time you stub your toe?

How many of your computer problems can be made that minor?

Mine are.

Appendices

Appendix 1 –

The Case for Buying a New Computer, And What Type to Buy

The easiest and best time to perform the setup Process we are describing is when you buy a new computer. It becomes much more awkward later, after the computer has been in use for some time, because two things will have happened: some amount of degradation will have occurred, and the hard drive will be partially full of user files. These two facts complicate our process.

The following recommendations for your new computer are based on some years of experience buying computers for myself and my customers. These recommendations are, of course, my personal opinions only.

First of all, my personal opinion is to not buy a mass-produced computer, although frankly the prices on these are excellent. I recommend getting what is called a "white box" computer, which means one built custom for you by a local reputable computer shop. They are typically in white or beige boxes, thus the name. This will cost you more than a comparable mass-produced machine, but there are several advantages:

1. Partitioning

When you have your machine built, you can have the builder partition the hard drive into two or more partitions. This is the most technically complex (and for the average computer user the scariest) part of this process, and your new machine will arrive with this partitioning already done.

2. Complexity

You want as clean and simple an installation as possible.

Mass vendors have a support problem. When tens of thousands of individuals buy a machine, many if not a majority of those users will be novices, and will get into various kinds of trouble while using their machines. The layout of a mass-produced machine is intended to make it physically possible to support millions of machines in this environment.

To this end, many of these vendors have "hidden" partitions on their hard drives which contain mirror images of the original manufacturer installation, just as we have described. Thus, if a user machine gets corrupted badly enough, the customer support person can talk them through a restore back to original factory condition. Often this is the only practical thing the vendor can do.

These arrangements, while good for the mass manufacturer, can cause unnecessary complexity in achieving what we're trying to do, particularly in the re-partitioning of the hard drive.

3. Bulk

In addition, these mass-produced computers typically arrive with a variety of additional software installed – various greeting card makers, music software, photo album software, "organizer" software, and the like. They commonly have "my shopping" type software (wonderful things we want you to buy!). They are typically loaded with such additional packages. These may or may not be useful to you, and make the original installation unnecessarily bulky.

It is often difficult to tell which of these applications may be removed. Are they unnecessary fluff (greeting card maker) or are they a required part of the installation, containing drivers for custom hardware?

It is difficult to know.

By buying a white-box machine, you will be getting a known entity, with exactly the software you have ordered, the necessary drivers, and nothing more.

4. Long Term Maintenance

There will be times when Windows requires you to insert your XP installation disk. Many of these mass-produced machines come with various CDs, but do not include an actual XP disk itself. This makes some maintenance details troublesome down the line.

An Example

As an example illustrating the above points, during this writing I set up a brand-new machine for my sister. It was, all in all, a very nice machine. It had a fast 2.3 GHz processor, a huge hard drive, Windows XP, a DVD reader and CD reader/burner, and some other really nice hardware. It came with four slots for flash media cards, memory sticks and so on, so that such things as a digital camera memory card could be inserted directly into the machine. It was $599 for the entire machine, including monitor and printer. All in all, it was a very nice machine, and in my opinion quite a good price.

However, it fit the characteristics I mentioned above. It came with all kinds of organizer, advertising, and other unnecessary software installed, and dozens of games.   I removed all of the "fluff" I felt I could safely deal with, including Blasterball, Slyder, Otto, Polar Bowler, and the like. However, even after removing all of the software that I could feel comfortable removing, the C: drive still contained 4.3 Gigabytes of files, and my sister had not yet installed her email and office software.

As a point of reference, the working drive on my main machine, complete with XP Pro, an email client, an FTP client, software development packages, a full Microsoft Office installation, some games, and several other applications installed, takes only 2.5 Gigabytes of space. To achieve this size I applied some techniques described in later appendices on setting up Windows, but mainly it has no "fluff" – I have installed all the application packages I need and nothing more.

This size matters.

As you do your imaging and restoring, the size of the data being imaged affects the amount of time it takes to do it. This has a practical impact, which I learned the hard way.

I was using earlier versions of Powerquest Drive Image a couple of years ago. I got a new machine, and bought and installed Drive Image on that machine. I had by this time gotten into the habit of doing this imaging Process to all my machines, so I started making images of the C: drive and routinely restoring. However, on this particular machine, for some reason the restore was taking 18 minutes, where on previous machines it had been on the order of two to three minutes. This 18 minute wait seemed like an eternity.

I got a nice and knowledgeable technical support person on the telephone, and she had me add a technical parameter to the program call. Now everything was back to normal, and restores took the appropriate two or three minutes.

I learned then that this restore time does matter.

If your restore time is two or three minutes, you will be willing to do it frequently. You fire up your restore, go get a cup of coffee, and come back and it's done when you get back from the coffee room.   Your machine is back to perfect.

If it is 18 or 20 minutes, it's entirely different. That's a very long time in the modern computing world to have your computer not available.

I found myself going quietly bananas waiting 18 minutes.

Therefore, a huge, bulky, loaded-up C: drive will make your restore time longer, and in practice will impact how often you are willing to do it. It will make the process an irritating annoyance instead of a routine and simple function.

By getting a white-box machine, you will get exactly what you need, and nothing more. If you decide you need photo-manager software or other functions, obtain and install that software.   If you want a few games, install them. But you will have nothing unnecessary on your machine, avoiding the bulk.   This makes for a cleaner environment, and facilitates long-term perfect operation.

How much size and horsepower?

Generally, get the cheapest. Most businesses do not need super-horsepower machines or enormous hard drives.

There is a tendency, when a machine becomes very sluggish (due to, say, adware or spyware or corruption) to think that a new machine with a faster processor is the solution.

However, Microsoft Word, Microsoft Excel, Internet Explorer, normal business application software, and ordinary email are not resource hogs relative to modern machine horsepower and size.   My experience is that the cheapest you can have built will be more than adequate for any normal business need.   If you are doing CAD or any graphics-intensive application, or if you are a "gamer", this of course isn't true for you.

General recommendations for my ideal business machine:

2 gigahertz processor or better

40 Gigabyte hard drive

256 megabytes of RAM (512 is better of course)

minimal video and audio

floppy disk drive (some mass produced machines are skipping this, but it is still   extremely useful)

Combination DVD burner/CD   burner drive (this is important)

Partitions:

C: drive 5 gigabytes or the smallest possible

D: drive all the rest of the available space

The last white box machine I bought with this layout cost $787.00.

There is an obvious common sense observation here – if you have, say, 20 or 30 gigabytes of music, movies, or some other large-file application, then modify this in the obvious manner.   Further, it would be recommended to partition your disk into three or more partitions, with, say, a large partition for holding all of your music or other large files.

Our goal, as described in Volume I, is to create maintain a pure (and relatively small) C: drive which contains the working programs, windows settings, and the Registry. It makes no sense to put large music or other files on that drive, thus inordinately increasing the imaging and restore time.

Operating System

Get Windows XP Home or Professional. As Windows 98 and Me will soon be non-supported, it is worthwhile to obtain a modern operating system. When the XP successor arrives, wait for the initial bugs to be ironed out (that is, wait for Service Pack 1 to be issued) and then move to that. All applications and networking are moving forward in technology and approach, and it is more trouble than it is worth to try to save a few dollars by remaining with an older operating system, with the hope that software builders backwards engineer properly, and the resulting frustration when it doesn't happen.

If you are legitimately in a position where you need to have Windows 98, then set up your machine with Windows 98 for old DOS functions or legacy programs you must have, with Windows XP in a dual-boot mode. I personally do this, as I am an old "DOS hound". But get XP for all your primary computing and networking functions.

Appendix 2 –

Setting Up Your Machine

If you have a new machine, or if you have restored your machine (see above) to original factory condition, we recommend some changes.

Out of the box, XP has settings which Microsoft has chosen. I make the following changes, all of which have one of two purposes:

1. to reduce the size of the windows working drive, usually C:

2. to make daily operation easier and clearer

Here are my recommendations:
a) Do not use System Restore. This will be replaced by the technique we are describing.

System Restore in Windows does a partial recovery when problems occur. It restores certain system files and settings to those that existed at a given restore point. However, it does not and cannot bring a machine back to perfect condition in the manner we are recommending. To do so would overwrite and wipe out any recent work on the C: drive. As this is unacceptable, it is only a partial restore.

Not using System Restore (assuming you are applying the process recommended in this book of course) will save noticeable space on your hard drive.

To select this option, right-click on My Computer and select "Properties". Under the System Restore tab, click "Turn off System Restore on All Drives." Click "Apply".

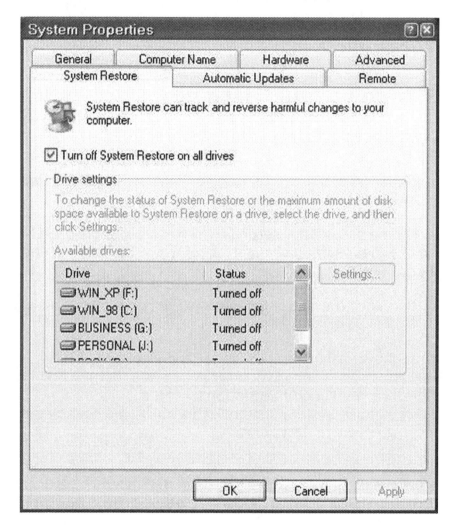

Turn off System Indexing. This is a space and CPU hog, with nebulous benefits. Right-click on My Computer and select "Explore". Now right-click on the C drive and select "Properties". You will see this screen:

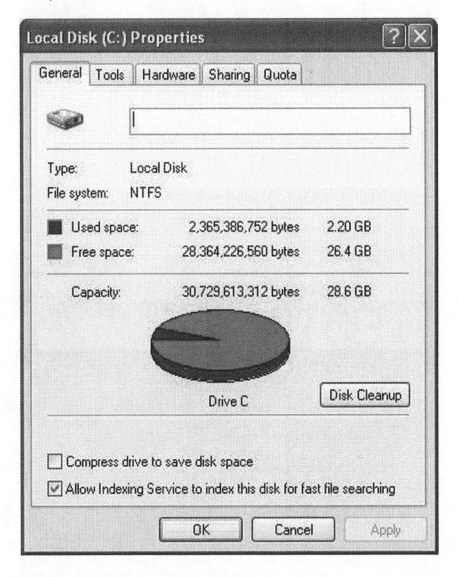

Now uncheck the Allow Indexing Service entry and click "Apply". The system will take a minute or two to clear out the present indexes. The next screen will be:

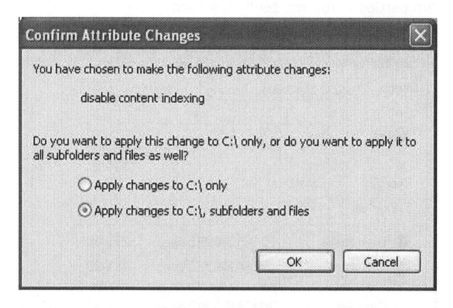

Select the second option as shown, and click OK. Along the way, this screen will appear:

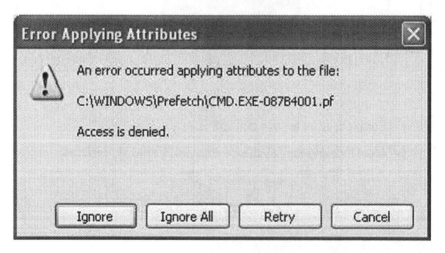

Select Ignore All – this simply means that some files require indexing by the system, and the un-indexing may not be applied. This is ok.

b) Turn off the Hibernate Feature. This is another space hog (it creates a very large hibernate file), and I don't use it.

To do this, click on Start-Control Panel or Start-Settings-Control Panel and double click on Power Options.

There may or may not be a Hibernate tab, as in this picture (some machines do not come with this option). If it is there, you will see:

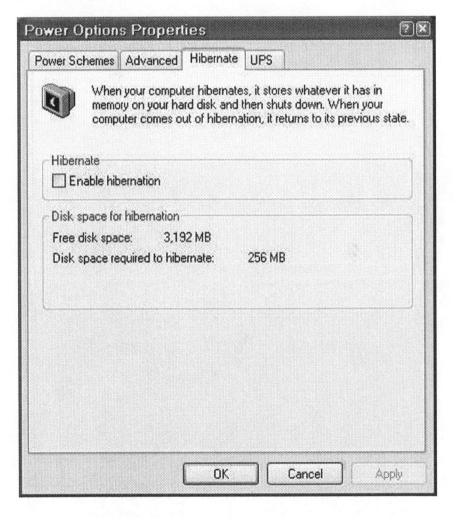

If the tab is there, un-check "Enable Hibernation", and click Apply.

d)   Later, after partitioning the drive, place the XP pagefile on a different drive from the one on which XP is installed.   The pagefile is a temporary memory "swap" file used by the system when your physical memory (e.g., 256 Megabytes of RAM) is full, and is typically hundreds of megabytes. There is no need to include this temporary file in your imaging process, thus artifically increasing its size.

To do this, right-click on My Computer and select Properties. There is an Advanced tab, as in this picture:

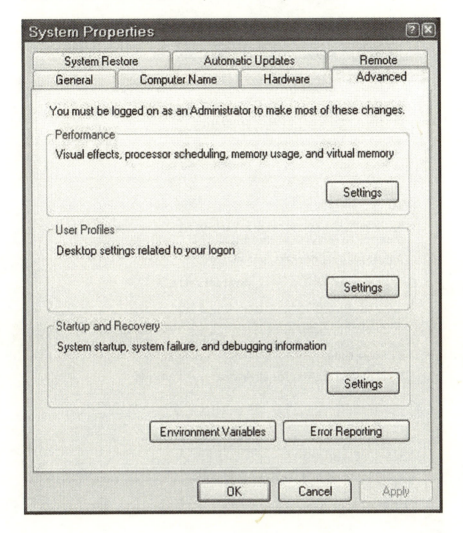

Now click on the first Settings button, under Performance. Now click the Advanced tab. You will see this screen:

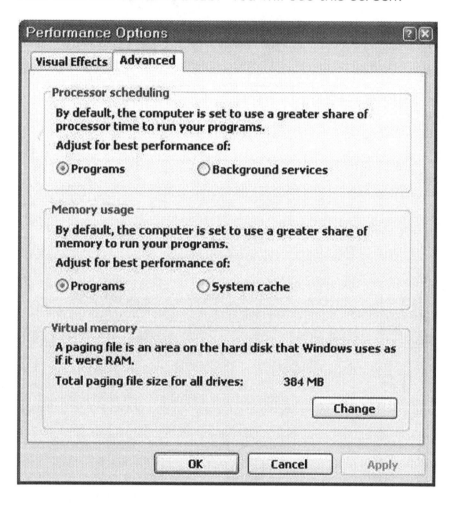

Click on the Change button under Virtual memory. You will see a screen much like this:

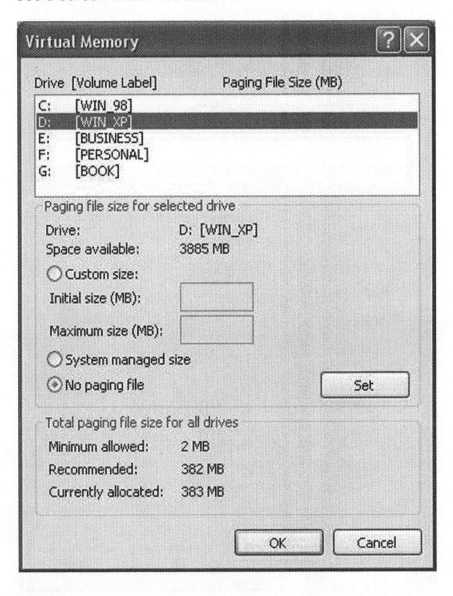

This is my machine, with five partitions, or "drives". Windows XP in this setup is operating from the D drive. When the D drive is highlighted, notice that it is saying "No Paging File."

Now highlight one of the other drives, and click on System managed size. This tells the system to place your pagefile on that drive, as here:

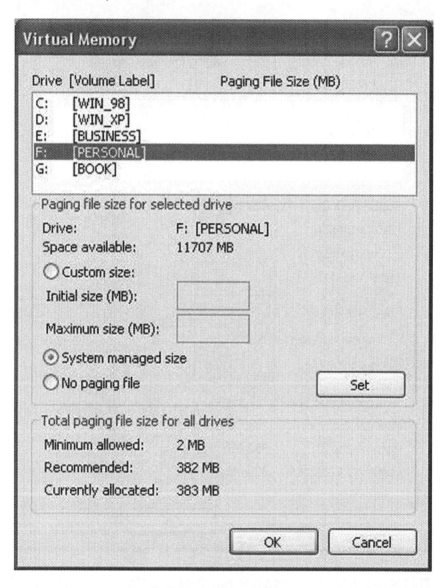

Now click "Set", select OK, and reboot your machine. This will move the XP pagefile to an alternate drive. Verify that the pagefile has actually been moved by using the Search function to search for "pagefile", and making sure that the file has actually moved after your reboot.

On my machine this paging file is about 400 Megabytes. There is no need to put that file on the drive which we will routinely be imaging and restoring. This is one of the primary goals of many of these recommendations: to minimize the amount of hard disk space that XP uses, as we will be making an "image" of that installation.

Appendix 3 –

More Windows Setup Recommendations

Microsoft, when building an operating system such as Windows, faces a fundamental problem. As a software developer for the last 30 years, I know the problem well, and it is this: you have to build a system which is simultaneously usable by a complete novice but which also has the flexibility and power to satisfy the needs of the advanced user.

There is no way to satisfy both types of users simultaneously – on each screen or function the developer must make some choice as to layout, options, and defaults chosen. Therefore, Microsoft must make some initial assumptions and defaults which are set when Windows is delivered, and these assumptions and defaults represent compromises. In general, the compromise leans towards the novice user, in an attempt to keep that user out of trouble as much as possible, assuming that the advanced user can modify these initial settings as required.

The downside of this approach, necessary though it seems to be, is that many initial Windows default settings are cumbersome, awkward, unnecessary, and in fact downright destructive for most computer-literate users attempting to perform actual work.

During my years in the software business I have spent much time doing direct customer support in many routine and complex situations, in addition to helping many of my friends with their computing problems (we computer nerds like to help folks!). I have learned a lot about how to make Windows usable, and much of it comes down to some very small things which cause a huge amount of difficulty for average users.

This section may seem to be over-focus on small settings, but my experience is that making these changes will smooth out your operation significantly over time, in addition to making the image requirements smaller and quicker.

Here we go, in gory detail.

General preliminary note: Whenever we say "right-click" we mean to click with the right mouse button. If we say anything else, such as "click" or "select", then we automatically mean the "normal" or left mouse button. (Obvious observation: reverse these instructions for left-handed users who have modified the mouse).

Classic View

Windows comes pre-loaded with a standard "user friendly" view of various options when one clicks the Start button. My experience is that the "Classic View" is cleaner and easier to use.

Right-Click on the Start Button and then select Properties. If you have a fresh XP install, you will see this picture:

Select the Classic View, and then click Appy.

This will allow you to see something like the following when you click on the Start Button:

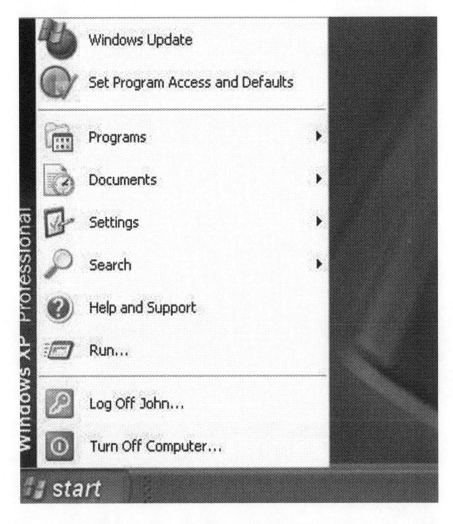

This classic view is much easier to navigate than the supposedly user-friendly view with which Windows XP comes installed.

Exposing All of Windows
Files and Extensions

Now right-click on My Computer and select Explore. You will see a screen such as the following on a fresh XP installation:

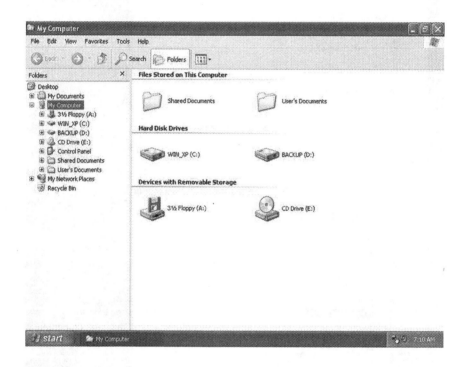

Note that Windows is fond of presenting you with little pictures. We will come back to this later. If you now click on the C: drive (marked WIN_XP C: on this particular machine), you will see this screen:

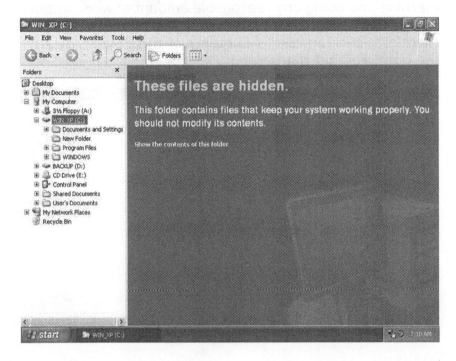

Microsoft, for some reason, thinks it is wise to hide the entire contents of the C: drive from the user. I suppose this is for "safety" reasons, so that a novice user does not mess things up. However, I cannot imagine you living with a machine and doing any reasonable amount of work without seeing and using the files on your machine. When you, therefore, click on "Show Contents of this Folder" over on the right, you get this screen:

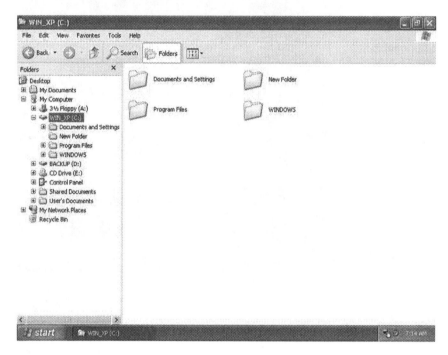

Good – we can now see some things on the C: drive. However, Windows by default hides a lot of things from you.

There are still some changes to make. As observed above, windows is fond of showing little pictures of things, I suppose so that you can see pictorially what's in a directory or "folder". This is fine when there are three or four items, but when there are even 20 or 30, this gets unwieldy. Therefore, we are going to switch to the "details" view of the folder.

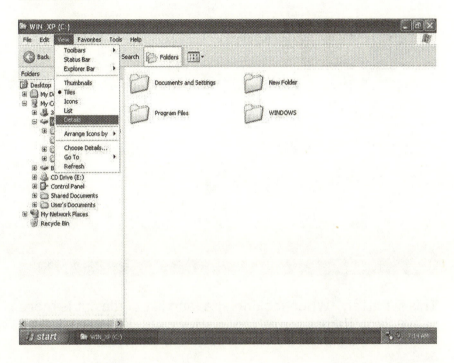

Click on View, and then Details.

Now you will see this:

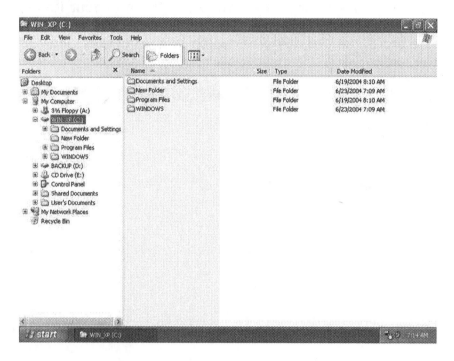

This is better.   When looking at a long list of files, it is more convenient than the pictures.   However, Windows is still hiding some things, so we make these changes:

Select Tools and then Folder Options. You will see this screen:

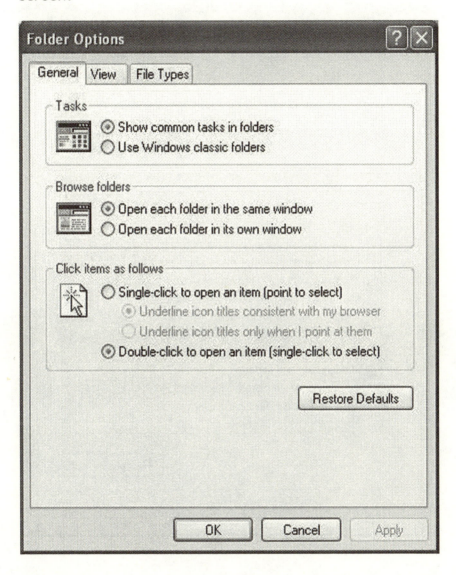

Now click on the View tab, and you will see this screen:

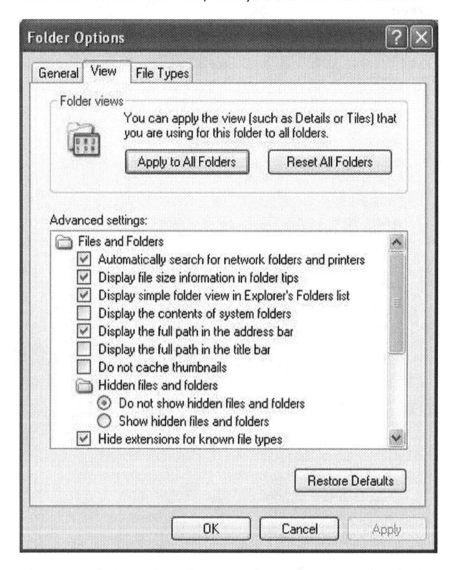

Make the following changes:

First, check the box by "Display the contents of system folders"

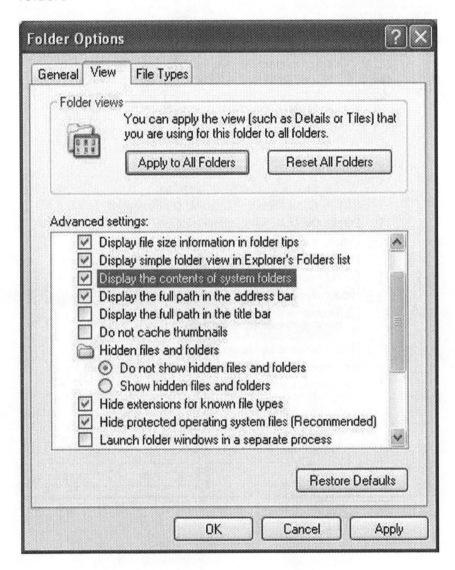

Now, check the button by "Show hidden files and folders".

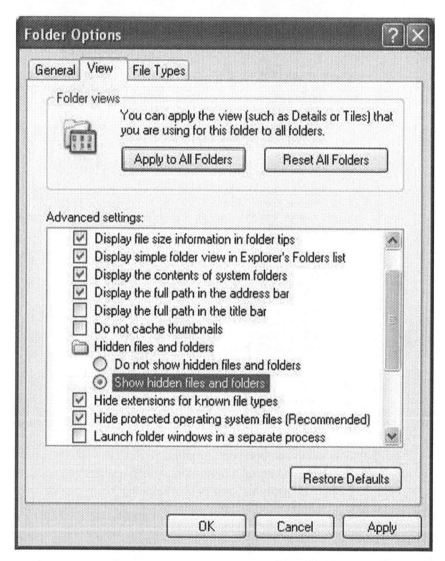

Now, UN-check the boxes by the entries "Hide extensions for known file types" and "Hide protected operating system files". We want to see everything!

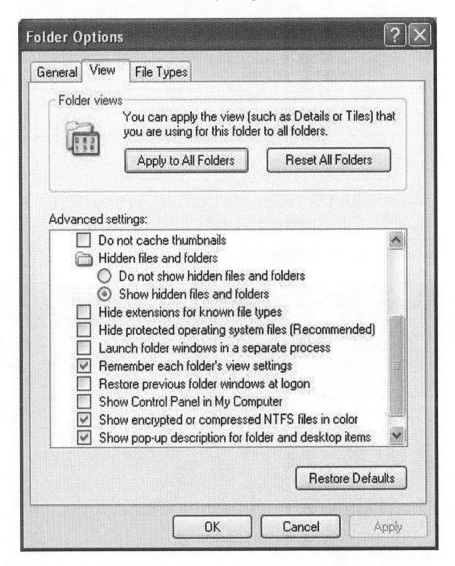

You will get this warning message:

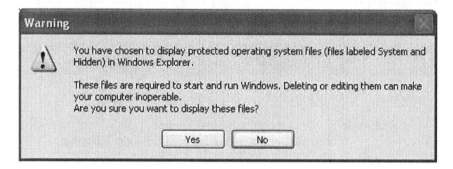

Click Yes.

Now click on the button up top that says "Apply to all folders".

You will see this screen:

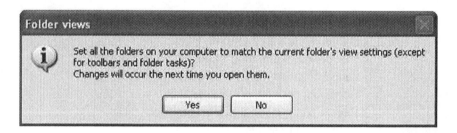

Clilck Yes, and then close out of the window. Your screen will now look something like this:

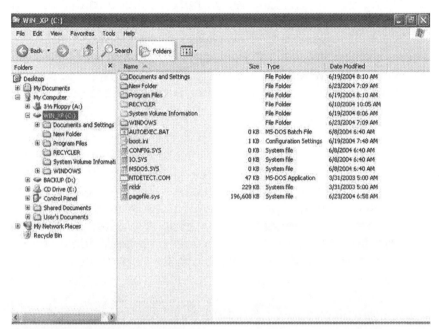

We can now see all the files on our machine, and see the entire file name.

Rationale

Hiding files from users may have a "safety" purpose, but is in general counterproductive.

Suppose that you are looking at the contents of a directory on your machine.

Without these changes you have some immediate questions:

Am I seeing all the files, or are some hidden? Am I looking at the entire file name, or is part of it hidden? What exactly is in this directory? If someone on the phone says "click on setup" and there are two "setup" files in front of me (extensions hidden) – which one do I click on? If someone is helping you on the phone, you are reduced to discussing what the "little pictures" look like.

These confusions are unnecessary. By setting as above, we can know that when we look at a list of files, we are seeing every file in the directory, and know that we are seeing the entire file name.

One of the most famous viruses was the Anna Kournikova virus, which spread by emailing a file named annakournikova.jpg.vbs. A "vbs" file is a "visual basic script" file, a program which can execute on your machine doing generally whatever it wants, and this particular one was a virus. However, since Windows has this default of "hide file extensions for known file types", a file with this name would appear to the user as

annakournikova.jpg   (hiding the "vbs" part of the fie name)

This appears to be a picture – most users know that a "jpg" is a picture. Millions of people double clicked on this "picture" to open it, only to have a virus program execute on their machine.

THE DESKTOP

One of the side effects of doing this process is that some things will be replaced (erased) by your image/restore process that you might not expect.

Three items in this category are

1. Your desktop

2. Cookies

3. Internet Explorer Favorites

The latter two take a bit of adjustment in terms of daily operation, but not much.

Erasing all your cookies will require, for example, that you re-enter your user id and password when entering certain sites, but that is the extent of the change. This adjustment is easy to make. The IE Favorites is similar – my Favorites list does not change frequently once I get my machine set up.

The desktop, however, is a bit more of a problem for one operational reason – many computer users use the desktop as a universal storage place, because it is easy to find.

Some users find the Windows file system confusing. Thus, if a user downloads a document or picture, placing it on the desktop makes possible to find later. This will not work if you apply this process, as the desktop will be brought back to its original condition every time you do a restore, thus losing anything stored there.

It is common for me to see friends' machines with 30 or 40 items or more on the desktop, since that is being used as the common storage area.

It will be necessary to change this part of your daily operation, if that is what you are presently doing. If the Windows file system is confusing to you, and if you are using the desktop in this manner, please study the Windows Primer in Appendix 4.

Question: If I do not use my desktop as a universal storage and retrieval point for my computer, what do I use?

An option is to use the My Documents folder, but the problem is that literally everything will end up in that folder, making it difficult to benefit.

Another problem is that unless you move the My Documents folder (as described in the Appendix on dealing with Microsoft Office), it is simply another folder on your C: drive, and thus will be replaced every time you do a restore. Our goal, recall, is to put all User Files and all variable information on alternate partitions, keeping only the working programs themselves on the C: drive.

What I do is this:

I create a folder on my alternate drive (say, for example, the D: drive) called something like "A_InOutBox".

I then use this folder as a universal temporary in/out transfer point for ALL files that I bring into or send from my machine.

Do not put this folder on your primary working drive which is imaged and restored, as that will be deleted every time we do a restore.

Why the name? Well, the "A" on the front brings it to the top of my file list when I do an explore of My Computer. Pictorially:

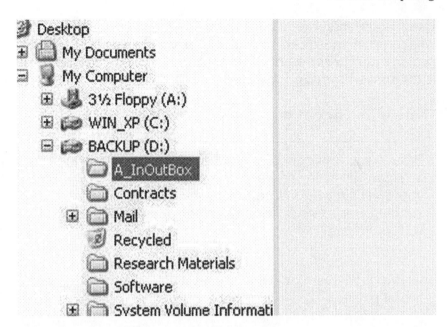

When I right-click on My Computer and select Explore, then this A_InOutBox directory shows as the first folder on my list on the alternate drive, in this case the D: drive. Thus it is easy to find.

When I download a file, I always put it there, decide what I want to do with it, and THEN move it to its ultimate destination. When I send an attachment out with an email, I copy that attachment to this A_InOutBox directory first. That way I can go to that directory and be VERY sure that I am sending the document or file that I think I am sending. Since it is the only document in that directory, then I *KNOW* later that I am attaching the correct item.

Have you ever sent the wrong document or wrong attachment by mistake?

Have you ever had two or three contract drafts running around, and needed to make VERY sure that you were sending the right one? Have you ever lost a contract or sale because you accidentally sent a draft with inappropriate comments in it for all to see?

Use of this universal in/out transfer point for your machine will remove the need to clutter up your desktop, and will provide clarity for all of your file transactions. I have used it for some time, and it works.

There is an obvious question here, and that is this:

> "You have described a process for partitioning and imaging, in order to keep the machine pure. Why are you spending any time whatsoever on such things as keeping the desktop clean? What does this have to do with anything?"

This is a good question, which really illustrates a fundamental general point.

We emphasized earlier in the Chapter 3 that there will be some rearranged use of the computer. There will be a fundamental change in the way you use your machine.

Imaging and restoring the C: drive will erase anything on your desktop. True, it is possible to "move" the desktop just as it is possible to move almost anything else in Windows, but this is not straightforward.

Much better, as we are recommending, is to learn to use your desktop and the C: drive only for things that remain stable, day after day, and learn to put all your documents and other variable User Files in some other folder in some other partition on your computer.

This will take some adjustment, but my experience is that it is well worth it.

You will have to learn how to navigate and use the Windows file system, and how to move files from one place to another in that file system.

As you use the computer on a daily basis, you must take the time and trouble to put things in appropriate places on the spot, rather than leave things on, say, the desktop.

Appendix 4 –

Applications With Unidentifiable User Files

We described in Chapter 13 how to identify the User Files for various types of Applications. There are two basic situations:

1. Some packages have User Files that are clearly recognizable. (See Chapter 14)

2. Other packages hide their files so deeply or tie their User Files together in such a complex manner as to make this method impractical for the average user.

A good example is America Online. I do not recommend America Online for business use, although I have recommended it to many of my friends for personal internet access, as it makes most internet functions as user-friendly as possible, and puts everything in one place. However, the files stored by America Online are not easily identifiable and movable in the way we want.

If you have America Online, or any other package in which you simply cannot figure out what the User Files are or where they are located, then we suggest a slightly modified process:

Practically all programs permit you to select where the software itself will be installed.

In this circumstance (where you cannot figure out what the User Files are or where they are located), what we recommend is that you install the entire program in your alternate drive as opposed to your working drive (typically the C: drive). Now your imaging will not contain the image of the software itself, but will serve the same basic functions we have been describing.

America Online, during the installation sequence, shows you this picture:

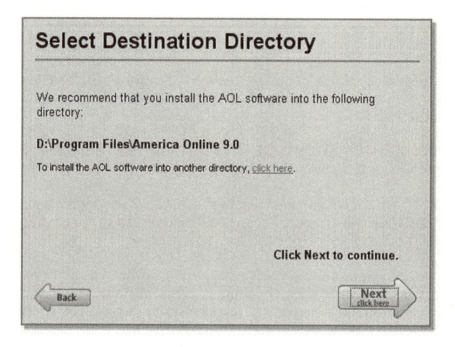

Clicking on the "To install the AOL software into another directory click here" link on this screen lets you select an alternate directory on your alternate drive for the installation of AOL, as in this picture:

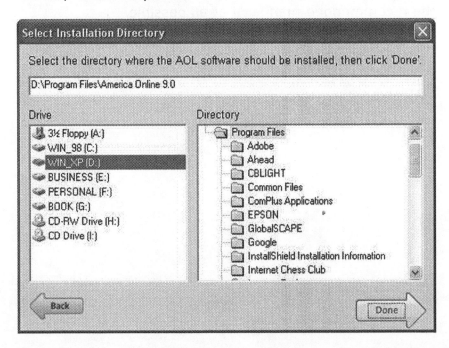

whereupon you can browse to a different location on your alternate drive for installation.

This alternate process removes the entire software application from the C: drive, which permits us to image and restore at will without affecting the User Data, which is our primary objective.

The downside of this alternate method is that it fails to facilitate another major objective of our Process, which is to make backing up your User Data very easy and quick, so that you do it more often.

If the number of packages installed in this alternate manner is small, and if many or most of them have integrated and good backup functions for their own User Files, this is feasible. It is better, in our opinion, to apply the process in the recommended manner if at all possible.

Appendix 5 –

The Windows File System, a Primer

If you are a relative novice with computers, the biggest single hurdle you will face is lack of understanding of the Windows file system, and how to manipulate files and folders inside Windows.

I have been personally doing customer assistance for users of my software for many years, and this lack of background is the biggest wall between the user and anything like full and effective use of their computer. Most individuals are never taught the basics of manipulating files and folders in Windows, and thus are limited to the "user friendly" interfaces which software builders attempt to create.

To say that these "user friendly" interfaces limit your productivity is a massive understatement – if there isn't a button or clearly-visible place to click for what you are trying to do (or if the language on that button isn't what you expect), you simply can't do it.

These "user friendly" interfaces are extremely limiting. The user, when using an application program, is typically unaware of the objects being created or used, what these objects are called, where they are being stored, and other fundamentals. This makes many tasks massively difficult.

For example, we have told you in the text to "back up your User Files" and to "remove your User Files from the machine." Without some basic understanding of Windows, these tasks are a near-impossibility.

Many otherwise experienced users have never had a clear explanation of this, which is one of the reasons the Desktop is used so frequently to store and retrieve files. I commonly see machines with 30 or 40 or more items on the desktop. Users save files or documents there, so that they can be sure to find them later, for the simple reason that the underlying file system is not understood, thus making it dangerous to put things anywhere else.

Windows doesn't help – many User Files are buried many levels deep in complex tree names. Outlook Express is a good example.

The mail files for Outlook Express on my machine are stored in a Folder with this name:

C:\Documents and Settings\John\Local Settings\ Application Data\Identities\{57CEFE09-2B0E-4C18-874A-70A84074845D}\Microsoft\Outlook Express

Huh? You have permission to scratch your head in confusion now......

> For those users who have never been taught these fundamentals on navigating and manipulating the Windows file system, this is a Primer.

From bottom to top, then, this is how the Windows file system is structured.

A Windows machine contains a large number of objects called "files". These files can be programs, data, pictures, songs, etc. They are contained in areas called "Folders" or "Directories". The files are kept in folders much like items are kept in folders in a filing cabinet.

The windows file system is like a house. A house has rooms. Inside each room is possibly two types of entities:

a) More rooms

b) Things

For example, inside the house you might have a living room. You go into the living room when you enter the house. In that room you see things (couch, TV, etc.) and doors to other rooms, such as bedrooms.

Going into the bedroom, you might see things (bed, TV, dresser, etc.) and doors to other rooms, such as a walk-in closet and bathroom.

Going into the bathroom, you might see things (razor, deodorant, etc.) and a door to another "room", like a pantry for towels.

If Windows Explorer were holding a house, it would look like this:

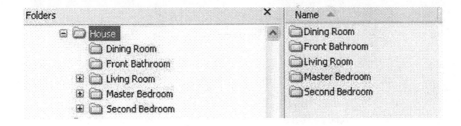

In this "house" we enter and see doors to the Dining Room, front Guest Bathroom, etc. The little plus sign to the left of the Master Bedroom means that there are other rooms inside that room. Now, if we enter the Master Bedroom (by clicking on it), we see a door to a walk-in closet (in effect another room) and a door to the Bathroom, together with a number of "things", such as a bed, bed stand, etc., like this:

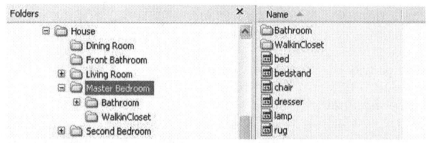

If we now enter the Bathroom, we might see a door to a storage pantry for towels and other items, and a number of "things", like a razor, shaving cream, etc.

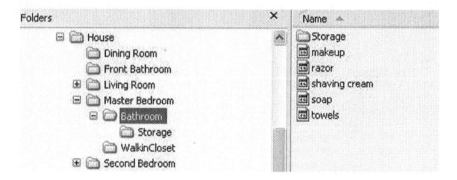

Windows is similarly set up.

The hard disk is initially delivered in most systems with a single label: the "C:" drive, which contains the entire contents of the hard disk. Assume that we do as we are recommending, and divide the hard disk into two "partitions", and assume that these partitions are called "the C: drive" and "the D: drive".

Each of these "drives" or "partitions" is analogous to our house: Inside each drive are two types of things:

a)   Folders (analogous to rooms and often called "directories")

b) Files of various types (analogous to "things")

Inside each Folder is possibly

a) More Folders

b) Files

and so on. Ultimately, of course, you reach the end of the "tree", and reach a bottom level where the contents of a Folder has no more folders, but only Files. A folder can be empty, just as a room can be empty.

Folders are also called "directories".

Right-click on My Computer and select Explore.

You are now looking at Windows Explorer, not to be confused with Internet Explorer.

The first thing you will see will be something like this (this is my main machine). Your machine may or may not have partitions like C:, D:, etc. It will always have a C: partition.

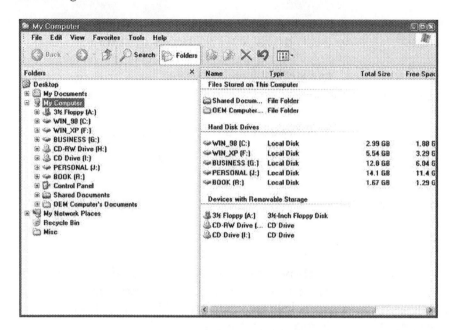

If there is a "plus" sign by My Computer, click on that plus sign. The "plus" sign on the left of any item indicates that there are folders underneath that part of the tree.

You are looking at the entire computer.

What we are doing is "exploring" My Computer.

This is my main machine. You will see several different "drives" or "partitions": a C: drive running Windows 98, an F drive running Windows XP, and so on. Clicking on a "plus" sign changes it to a "minus" sign, and shows the folders underneath, like this:

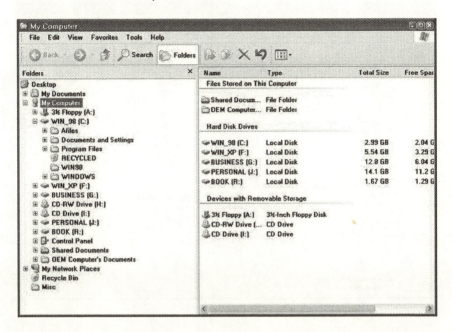

Thus, inside the C drive you see some folders: Documents and Settings, Program Files, Windows, and so on.

Clicking on the small plus sign by the "Program Files" folder, Windows Explorer expands the view to show all the folders underneath "Program Files." There are folders for Accessories, Microsoft Office, and so on.

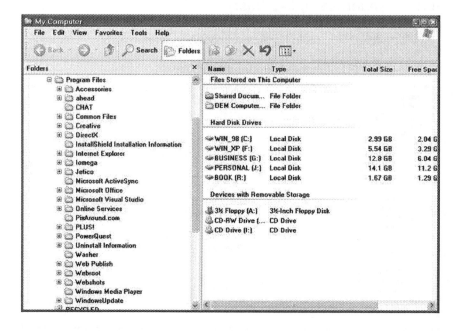

If, now, you click on any one of those subfolders, the right side of Explorer will show you the contents of that folder. For example, here I have clicked on the Webshots folder (what I use for my screen saver). Inside that folder, notice, are two things: more Folders and some files, with the Folders indicated by a small picture of a file folder, and every other "thing" showing an icon depending on the type of file:

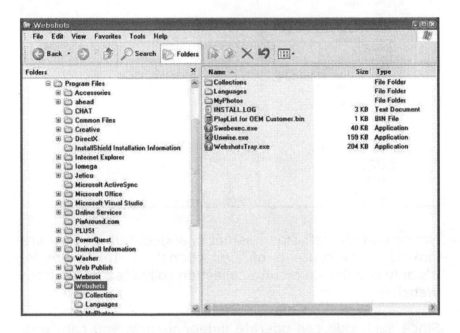

When we say to "browse" to a certain place, we mean to go "down the tree" until you get to the desired location. You do that by clicking on the appropriate folder name, then the appropriate subfolder name, etc. until you get to the folder you wish to be in.

The two halves of Windows Explorer can operate independently of each other.

This is very useful for moving files from one place to another.

If, for example, we wish to see the contents of the "Collections" subfolder of Webshots, but wish to leave the left half of

Explorer as is, we double-click the Collections folder in the RIGHT half of Explorer, resulting in the following picture:

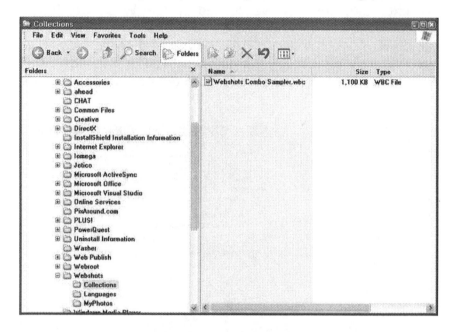

Notice that the left side has not changed, but we now are looking at the contents of "Collections". In this example, it's only one file – a picture collection called "sampler" from Webshots.

Since each side can operate independently, you can, with some practice, get to where you can see any folder or directory on the left side, and any file anywhere on the machine on the right.

Thus, when we say "move a file from A to B", the process is to browse right until you see the file in question, and then browse on the left until you see the directory which is the target. Then, using the RIGHT mouse button, drag and drop that file from the right side of Explorer to the target directory on the left side.

When you are moving a file from one place to another on your hard drive using Windows Explorer, be sure to drag the file from one place to another using your RIGHT mouse button.

In some circumstances, if you drag using the left mouse button, Windows will appear to move the file, but will actually only make a shortcut. This will cause you infinite confusion. Therefore, always move a file with the RIGHT mouse button. You will then get a drop-down menu asking if you want to copy the file or move the file, and it will then be clear what you have done.

In general, learn to use the right mouse button. Try clicking on various things with the right mouse button, and see what options appear. "Delete", "Rename", and "Properties" are things which will be very useful over time, and live under the right mouse button.

Making a New Folder

Occasionally during this manuscript we have directed you to create a new folder for some purpose, typically as a new location for your User Files.

Here is how to do it.

Suppose we wish to create a new folder called Temp inside the Program Files folder in the C: drive. Right-click My Computer and select "Explore" as usual, and then click on the C: drive so that you can see the folders on the C: drive. A picture will appear something like the following:

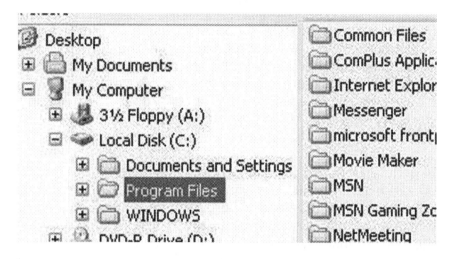

Click one time on the Program Files directory, and it will then be highlighted as indicated in the picture. Now select File – New – Folder as in this picture:

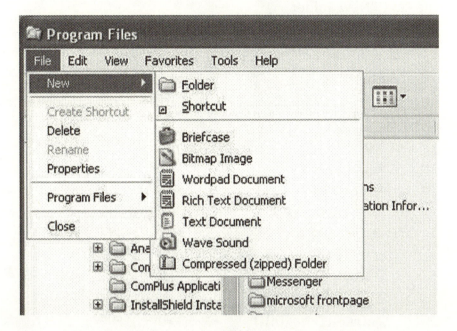

John Bridges

Now, Windows will add a new folder in a box on the right side
of the screen, with the title New Folder. It is highlighted,
so that when you start typing whatever you type replaces
the text "New Folder".

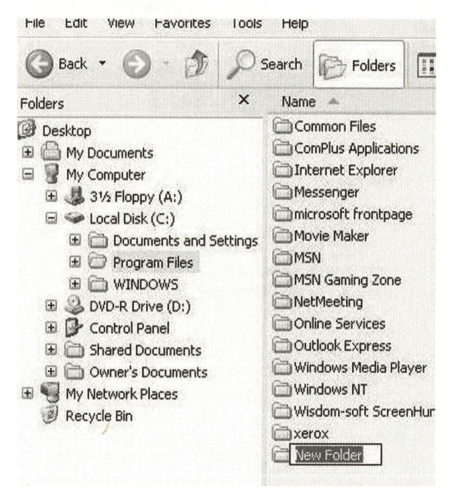

Now type the word "Temp" and hit Enter.
The system will replace the text "New Folder" with the word
Temp and show you your new folder, like this:

Browsing with the File-Open
and File-Save As Functions

As we discussed in Appendix 1, you may use the File-Open and File-Save As functions in many applications to open files and save files anywhere on your computer. If you are unfamiliar with this "browsing" process, here is how it looks. This set of examples is done using Microsoft Wordpad, a utility on all Windows machines.

When you click on File, you will see a set of options. Click on Save As:

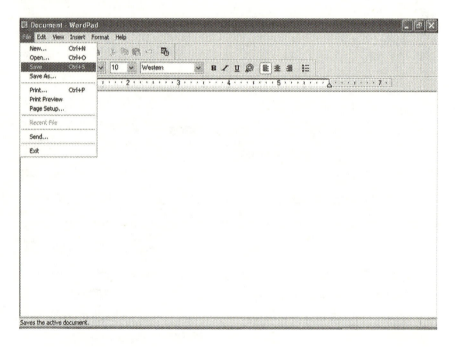

You will see a screen similar to the following. At the top, you see a "Save in" box, with a default (My Documents in this case) and an arrow. If you click on the arrow in that box, you get a layout similar to the one shown in Windows Explorer, but without showing any of the files. You are not shown the files, but only the folders or directories. This is because the system only wants to know where you want to put the file when you save it. Clicking on the arrow gives you something like this:

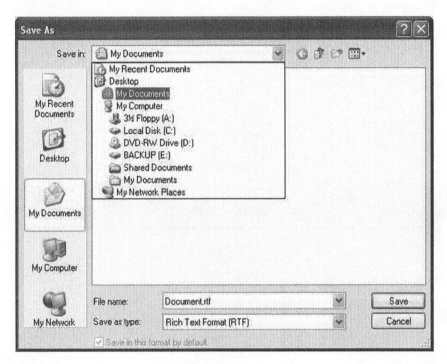

If, as in this example, your alternate drive is the E: drive, clicking on that gives you a picture similar to this:

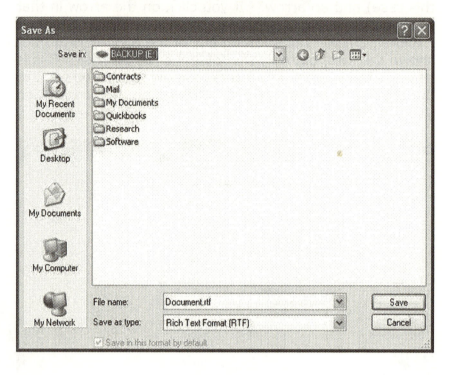

If now we double click on, say, the Research folder:

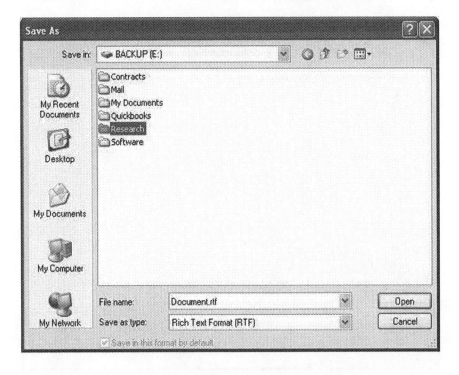

you will see that folder and any of its relevant present contents:

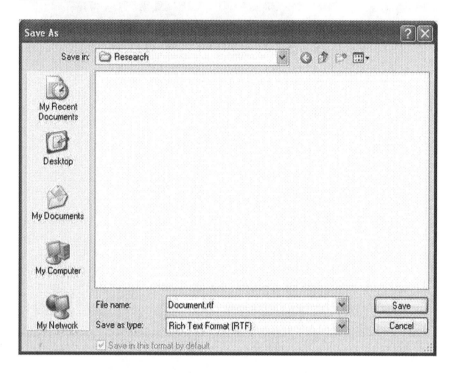

By "relevant present contents", we mean that Windows shows you all of the files in that folder which are of the same type as the one you are about to save. In this case, there are apparently no other ".rtf" documents in that particular folder. If there were others already there, you would see them.

Similarly, clicking on File-Open

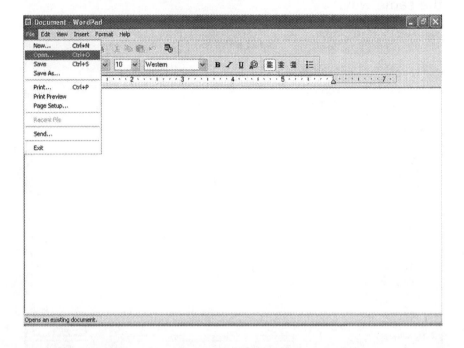

gives you an identical series of screens, which operate in the same way.

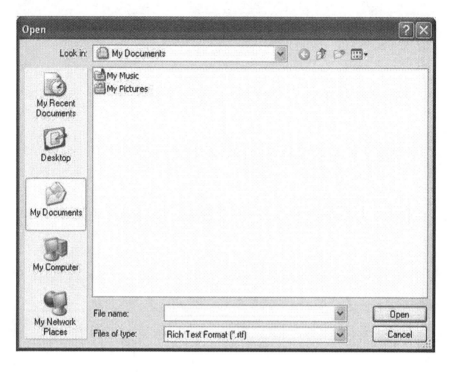

Clicking on the arrow by "My Documents" (the default open folder in this case) gives you a picture exactly as in the File-Save As sequence:

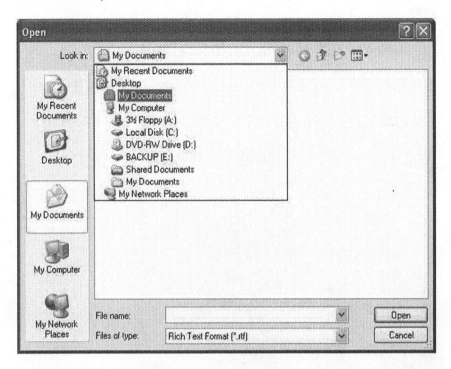

It is worth your while to practice until you are comfortable navigating and "browsing" the hard drive on your computer.

Using the Windows Search Function

Sometimes you don't know where your User Files are, or the files are buried too deeply to be easily found. The Outlook Express example given above is a good one.

We will show you here a common sequence using the Windows Search function, in which we search for a file (or files) and then move that file to another location.

We take as an example the situation above with Microsoft Outlook, where we told you to find and move the file

outlook.pst

which contains all of the outlook address books and email files.

Suppose you don't know where this file is.

You can use the Windows search function to find the file.

Click on Start then Search, seeing the following screen:

Click on All files and folders, giving you:

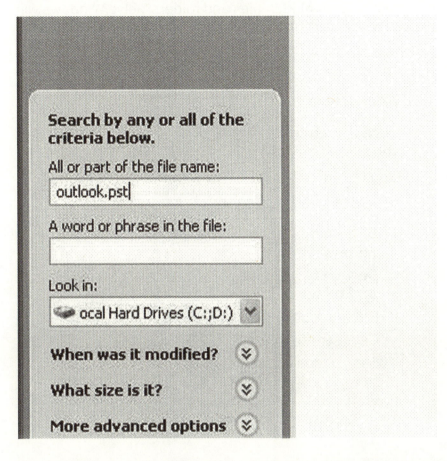

Now, type the name of the file into the box labeled "All or part of the file name".

Be sure, under the "More advanced options", that you have selected "Search hidden files and folders", else Windows will not show you certain system files, as we discussed above:

Now, clicking on Search permits Windows to find the file outlook.pst:

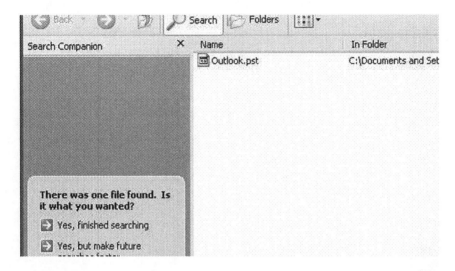

Now, leave this window open, and explore My Computer as we have discussed, opening a separate Window:

John Bridges

In this case we have previously created a folder called Mail on our alternate drive, in this case the D: drive:

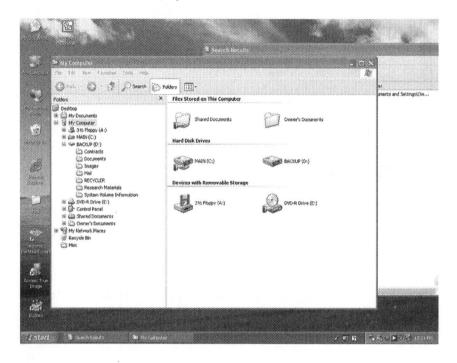

Now, move the windows around so that you can see both the file we are moving on the right, and the target director on the left, like this:

Now, using the RIGHT mouse button, click on the outlook. pst file and drag it over to the Mail folder we created, and then release the mouse button. This is called "dragging and dropping" a file.

You will get a menu like this:

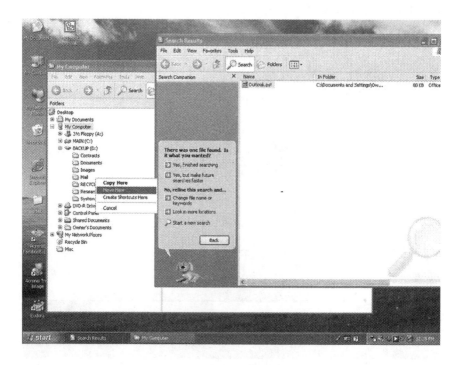

Windows is now asking you what you want to do with the file you have just moved. The two most important options are "Copy Here" and "Move Here". In this case, we wish to select "Move Here", moving the outlook.pst file to its new location.

Note: the "*" character is a wild card. Thus searching for "outlook.*" will find any file with the name "outlook" and having any extension. Searching for "*.doc" will find all Word documents, and so on.

www.ingramcontent.com/pod-product-compliance
Lightning Source LLC
Chambersburg PA
CBHW051234050326
40689CB00007B/916